An Immigrant's Journey

by

Mark Iutcovich

with the assistance of

Chris Dubbs

RIVERCROSS PUBLISHING, INC.
New York • Orlando

Printed in the United States of America. No part of this book may be used or reproduced in any manner whatsoever without written permission, except in the case of brief quotations embodied in critical articles and reviews. For information address RIVERCROSS PUBLISHING, INC., 127 East 59th Street, New York, NY 10022

ISBN o-944957-71-4

Library of Congress Catalog Card Number: 97-8585

First Printing

Library of Congress Cataloging-in-Publication Data

Iutcovich, Mark.
    An immigrant's journey / by Mark Iutcovich.
      p.   cm.
    ISBN 0-944957-71-4
    1. Iutcovich, Mark. 2. Romania—Politics and
government—1944-1989. 3. Romania—Politics and government—1989-
4. College teachers—United States—Biography. 5. Sociologists-
-United States—Biography. 6. Refugees, Political—Romania-
-Biography. 7. Refugees, Political—United States—Biography.
I. Title.
DR267.5.I93A3   1997
949.803'092—dc21   97-8585
                                                                 CIP

Dedicated to my Wife Joyce and my daughters, Mara and Nadia.

An Immigrant's Journey

Preface
An Immigrant's Journey

Spring 1950. Bucharest, Romania.

I sat in the office of the Secretary of the Communist Youth Organization, occupying a chair that faced his empty desk, waiting, struggling with my imagination. I had been summoned and had no idea why. I was not a member of the Communist Party and had done nothing wrong. Still, it was a strange time, and one could do wrong without even knowing it.

I was near the end of my senior year of studies at the University of Bucharest, set to strike out on my adult life, but I had no place to go. Two years before, my family home, farm, and business had been nationalized, and my parents fled the country. Romania had been refashioned in the five years since the Red Army occupied the country at the close of the War, and in the few years since the Communist Party took firm control of the government. In big ways and small, life in Romania had changed to such a degree from my childhood as to be nearly unrecognizable.

I had seen Marxism creep into the curriculum at the university, watched as independent-minded professors disappeared from the classroom, tried to reason with passionate friends who fled to the mountains to fight with the anti-communist partisans, and struggled to keep focus on completing an education that I now thought to be nearly worthless. I had been unable to reconcile myself to these changes. And now I wondered if I would ever travel, with all the baggage from my past, into the new Communist future.

The door behind me opened, and a man appeared. The Secretary would be delayed, he said. I felt a gentle heartthrob quicken in my chest, certain that this was a calculated delay to make me squirm. But why?

I had come from a bourgeois family, my father a capitalist land owner. We had operated a lucrative business and lived in a fine house with servants. I myself had been scheming, ever since my parents left the country, for a way to make my own escape. I had refused to join the Party, and within the university had made no secret of my resistance to Communism. It took no great leap of imagination to think that I might be in some jeopardy.

When I had tortured my way through this reasoning a dozen times, the Secretary finally appeared with a file folder which he opened on his desk. His movements were abrupt. He was a busy man who needed to dispense with this business quickly. "We are quite pleased with your record, since you opposed the Nazis," he began. "However . . . your parents and your background . . . they are not ideologically sound."

Just like that, the whole of my life had been reduced to that one evil phrase, "not ideologically sound." The Secretary's expression invited my defense. Though I had never met him, his face was familiar to me from the newspapers. His name was Nicolae Ceausescu, and he would one day have his dictatorial reign as Romania's president. In 1950 he was already a man of considerable power, with a ruthless reputation, who had now turned his attention to my ideologically-deficient family. It was no idle observation; people had been punished for lesser offenses.

My heartbeat now sounded in my ears, but I gave no outward reaction to his statement. The last decade of life in Romania, under fascists and Communists, had made me a master at concealing emotions when I chose to. And, of course, I had no defense to offer against this charge.

Then a weak smile pressed onto his lips, seemingly at the satisfaction of making me nervous. "However, I have not called you here to discuss that but to open the door of opportunity," he said. "We would like you to take charge of the Communist Youth Newspaper, to edit it, to build it in size and influence. This is a wonderful opportunity for you."

So, this is the way careers were made, I thought. The Romanian Communist government was only a few years old: embrace the faith and you could rise swiftly. I had seen it happen with some of my friends.

Still, I needed no time to consider his offer. All the thinking I had done on the subject of Communism had long taken place. My answer was brief and to the point, diplomacy never being my strong point. "I cannot undertake the assignment because I do not share your ideology. Besides, I do not like foreign boots on my country's soil."

A more rational man would have taken the offer, realizing that Communism was in Romania to stay, and therefore required accommodation. But, the moment seemed to instantly engulf my young life as an event of profound importance, a turning point, where my allegiance would go on record.

I was 20 years old at the time, and half of my life had been spent with a foreign power occupying my country. The Soviet occupation at that time was as loathsome to me as had been the German occupation during the War, the Communist ideology as unpalatable as that of the Nazis. I had witnessed first hand the psychology of complacency that grips individuals, an entire country, allowing totalitarian regimes to seize control. I wanted no part of this offer.

It was more irritation than anger that registered on Ceausescu's face. He was obviously a man who usually got his way. He had led the collectivization of agriculture in Romania, killing thousands in the process. So, one stubborn student was not a problem. He did not waste his time arguing with me.

I assumed that my decision would have consequences, but I did not appreciate how quickly they would befall me. Within weeks, I was arrested. It took only minutes for a legal committee to process my case and commit me to a prison camp. Thus began my stint in Romania's *gulag*, where tens of thousands of my countrymen went to be "re-educated" or to die.

That fateful moment in Ceausescu's office looms so large in my memory, because it was a point from which there was no turning back. I spoke my convictions and lived with the consequences. But many other moments had preceded that one in shaping my thinking. Romania's Iron Guard and its fascists, the Nazis and the Communists, had provided moments in abundance to carve my animosity in stone. I had witnessed brutalities and experienced the poisonous effects of mistrust and suspicion that take root in a repressive society—manipulation of the truth, the construction of the false reality, the whole house of cards on which such societies are built.

Now this criminal government had criminalized my resistance. I entered the prison camp at Pereprava, not knowing the length of my sentence. From before dawn until after sunset, we labored like draft animals building dikes in the Danube delta. Those like myself, who did not succumb to exhaustion, starvation, malaria, or the cold, were transformed by the experience.

Upon my release from Pereprava, I wanted more desperately than ever to leave my country, for it had changed as much as I had changed. The once flourishing economy, the lively culture, and the cheerful people that I remembered from before the war, had all but disappeared. Even the comparison to three years earlier was shocking, even more life having been wrung from the country.

But, I would live five more years in Communist Romania, in a strange land that was but a ghost of its former self. Working as a planner in a planned economy, helping to construct the fiction of Romania's economic advance, I clung to the dream of one day escaping the country.

"Do you know who this is?" a voice said on the phone one day in 1958. I recognized it immediately as that of a childhood friend then in a high government post. Ten years earlier, he had refused to help me leave the country, and I had not spoken to him since. In a cryptic exchange right out of a John le Carre spy novel, he explained it was urgent that we meet. One simply assumed that other ears shared every phone conversation, and so names were not mentioned, nor was the reason for his call.

We met like spies in a park. A pending shakeup in the government would likely cost him his position, he explained. He wished to make this final gesture of friendship while he still could. He handed me a false passport and wished me well.

There was great risk associated with an attempt to leave the country with false papers. I might be returned to prison, a prospect that chilled me. But I could not have been more ready to risk life itself to escape. One harrowing train ride took me to freedom. After twelve years, I was reunited with my parents in Canada.

Capitalism, I would discover, had its own set of hurdles and its own predatory individuals. My father, who had survived encounters with Nazis and Communists, lost his considerable fortune to the first unscrupulous businessman he met in the New World. He was too old to rebuild his fortune, but at age 30, I started life over.

Building a life in America followed a rocky road; I had many lessons to learn. Some of the qualities I brought from the Old World got me into trouble in the New World. But, I also I came to learn that other qualities I brought from my past served me well. A love of learning dictated my career choice. The gambler's spirit and freewheeling capitalism learned at my father's knee laid the foundation for financial success. A university professorship and the founding of a research institute have brought me satisfaction and material comfort.

I think of myself as a survivor. Even now, with the blessing of a loving family and financial security, I am always wary. Everything can be lost or taken away. I have seen it happen too often to doubt this.

Perhaps because I have lived through several monumental shifts of government and suffered their consequences, I am conditioned now to pay special attention to politics. Unlike people who have lived under a stable political system their whole lives, I take nothing for granted. Unlike people who think a repressive government could never rise up in their favored country, I watch political developments very carefully. Because I know it can happen.

And frankly, occurrences in Washington often scare me. Too much power going to one political party, erosion of personal liberties, politicians and political-interest groups that reduce complex political questions to one emotional issue—these trends have ushered in the Age of the True Believers, those who strive to gain power and set the agenda for the country, convinced they know what is best for all of us.

These are but a few of the things that strike a nerve in me. They dredge up painful memories of events from my youth, when step by step the march towards totalitarianism went unopposed. They make me passionately concerned with politics and an active supporter of candidates.

All of these things from the past that have shaped me have lain hidden from everyone, even my family, so much so that I often feel like two men in one body. Although my life has been lived in the context of much political turmoil, that political turmoil has also occurred in the context of my life. In writing this memoir, it is my life I mean to talk about more than history and politics. People and places, love, disappointment, tragedy, and joy. These are the meat of my memories and the basis of my life story. These are the things asking to be brought back to the light.

My present life in 1990s America rests uncomfortably beside its younger counterparts in the Romanian monarchy of the 1930s and the Romanian Peoples Republic of the 1950s. At once my early life seems so elemental a part of the man I am today, and yet it seems like a life lived by another, when the world was different, when the world was innocent and the world was mad.

My goal in writing these memoirs was not to hold my life up as example, not to win praise, be instructive, or make excuses. It was simply to chart my passage from that world to this. Also, I write to make this one life part of the record.

An
Immigrant's
Journey

1
In The Beginning

I can picture my father, Joseph Iutcovich, in 1921, standing in the blazing sun on the steppes of Bessarabia, watching his sheep nip at the roots of the parched grass. It was a year of terrible drought. The fertile black soil of the region had turned dusty brown, crops had shriveled, and the sheep had dropped weight.

He had a wife, a two-year-old son, and a restless spirit. I imagine him turning his gaze southward, towards the fertile Danube delta of Muntenia and feeling the gravitational tug that would make him leave his ancestral village for a new life in another province of Romania.

This event, before my birth, falls into the pre-history of my life, living now because my mother was a story teller. Her account of their move and their early years in their new home was retold often to her children. Incidents were refined, details added, misfortunes dramatized, until the story gathered a moral weight on a par with the biblical Exodus. The events became so familiar to me that I felt I too had been present, and they had left their mark on me. So, they seem a suitable place to begin an account of my life.

Of course, this small event in the history of my family was set against larger historical events. From the earliest recorded history, Romania had been embroiled in the sweep of wars, waves of colonization, and foreign political accords that redrew its national borders. The 20th century would be no different. Only at the close of World War I had Romania wrested Bessarabia back from Russia. Our ancestral homeland moved from the empire of Russia to the monarchy of Romania in time to escape the Bolshevik

Revolution. My maternal grandfather proudly displayed a medal he had received from King Ferdinand of Romania for services rendered to the Romanian Army during WW I. A Romanian general, staying in his home, had baptized my brother Leon. Grand events seemed to unfold like a mural in that part of the world, often shaping lives in harsh terms.

My parents moved from Bessarabia in 1921, the same year the Romanian Communist Party was officially established. It had announced its presence with strikes the previous year. My father was not an overtly political man. He would in later years be drawn into activities considered subversive, but he engaged in them not as an act of political defiance but rather for deeper reasons: loyalty to friends, common humanity, self-preservation, and perhaps, the more inscrutable motivation of Romanian nationalism.

By the time I was a child and gaining the first glimmering awareness of such things, the political stage was filled more with fascists than with Communists. But all of that came later. In my early years, these political storms stood removed from our lives. My earliest memories are of an idyllic existence—a loving mother, a strong, hard-working father, the company of two older brothers, and all the trappings of a well-to-do life.

I was born in 1929, the mid-point between the two great wars that would so disrupt life in Romania. Braila, where we lived, was a bustling, provincial city of some 70,000 souls. We owned a large house that had once belonged to a wealthy landowner. Five large rooms filled the first floor, bedrooms lined the second floor. I had the third floor all to myself, a single, spacious room tucked under the eaves, with a panoramic view of the front street and the barn behind.

Father owned a large farm outside of town. It was a huge operation, 300 hectares of land, with 10,000 sheep, 50 pigs, 50 cows, a grist mill, and a cheese making operation. It took about 60 workers to manage things. The output of the farm was sold to numerous wholesale and retail accounts. To supply meat for all these customers, Father was constantly dealing in cattle, driving to market towns throughout the region to buy livestock.

He owned an old Fiat automobile in those days and employed a chauffeur. The rattle of its engine sounded odd in a world where people and commerce still traveled mostly by horse. In all of Braila there were but a handful of automobiles, and a few taxis. Braila's better families still paraded their ornate carriages through the streets. The clip-clop of the horses' hooves on the dirt streets echoed of an earlier age, then in its twilight. It pleased Father to embrace the modern when it had such practical application.

Mornings, the grumble of the car engine would burst through my bedroom window. From there I could watch Nicu the chauffeur opening the car door, Father settling into the rear seat, and then the two of them chugging off for another cattle-buying excursion. To me, Father seemed a very important man, a step above other mortals.

"Your father is a gambler," my mother would say during her stories. Her tone of voice revealed that she admired this quality, just as she delighted in telling stories about the family, and about herself and my father. The stories would illuminate the personalities of my parents and relatives, but they imparted important moral lessons as well.

My brothers and I were an attentive audience who especially enjoyed hearing of the misfortunes our parents had endured. Most children like to tease themselves with horror stories and scary things. That may explain my fascination with these accounts. They revealed that family circumstances had not always been as good as they were, that things could change, quickly and calamitously.

"Your father made big money during World War I," Mother would tell us. My older brothers, who had heard these stories more times than I, would lend a respectful ear, but I would lean closer, intent on her words.

"France and Romania fought side by side in that war. Your father provided them with supplies. He would be away for a long time and then return with heavy boxes. 'Look what I have made,' he would say, holding up handsful of gleaming coins. We hid them under the bed. Boxes and boxes of gold. That is how he made his fortune."

She would tell us about their life in Bessarabia, their farm and their vast herd of sheep. Life was good. Then came the drought, drying the grasslands on which the sheep depended. So Father went in search of a new home, traveling south into the Danube delta.

It was not part of Mother's story, but I can imagine that, to a man coming from a land of drought, the delta must have seemed like a heaven-sent oasis. It is lush with brooks, lakes, marshes, and canals. Wildlife is abundant. Hundreds of species of birds stop there on their migratory journeys. The original inhabitants of the region were called the Daci, but twenty-five hundred years ago the Greeks settled there in the town of Tulcea, where the Danube first fans itself into a delta. The Romans followed them.

It must have been an easy decision for Father to follow their lead and adopt this lush area for his new home. Just north of Tulcea, to the city of Braila, my father brought his family to start a new life.

Then misfortune struck. The starving sheep, gorging themselves on the rich grassland, began to sicken and die. My oldest brother Leon was an infant then, living with my mother in Braila. Father stayed many kilometers away in the Delta on grassland leased from the government. The news coming from Father was not good. The sheep were dying by the hundreds, the thousands.

"In the winter, when your father returned home, he had a big beard," mother would say with gravity, for it signaled more than a change in shaving habits. "'We have lost everything,' he said. 'There are just enough sheep left to pay the workers, and that's it.'" They could not even pay the rent on their house.

But mother's stories never ended with misfortune. Disaster was only an obstacle to test one's character. The heart of the story was that Father began again, choosing to establish a cattle business this time. And again, ambition and hard work paid off. He became a very successful wholesaler of meat. This was the mid-1920s. My brother Misa had been born.

"We were well off then," Mother explained. "We had a nice house and servants. For someone else it would have been enough. But you know your father. Never satisfied. He tried the export business." If there was a hint of exasperation in her voice, it was overshadowed by tolerance and admiration for Father's accomplishments.

The export story was famous. It was one of my favorites. In 1926, Father invested nearly every cent he had in a venture to export cattle to Czechoslovakia. Father liked to think big and accomplish large projects. He bought up livestock throughout the region, nearly 1,000 head, and loaded them into train cars. He stood to make a considerable profit.

But when he arrived at the border, the laws had been changed, prohibiting the import of live cattle into Czechoslovakia. Undaunted, Father butchered 1,000 cattle on the spot and shipped in the meat. But, no refrigerated cars were available. By the time the plodding train reached Prague, the meat had spoiled.

"Your father was downcast when he returned home. 'My dear wife,' he said. 'This is all I have rescued from my business venture.' And he handed me a pair of silk stockings." It made Mother smile to tell it. It made my brothers and I smile, as well.

After more than half a century, that detail of Mother's smile still stands in my memory. There was more to the story that day, but recalling it now, it's hard to get past that smile. It gave more weight to Father's simple display of affection than to his business disaster. After all, money came and went, but love endured. Life might hand you a sea of troubles and setbacks, but the bonds of family sustained you.

Sometimes, in hindsight, it's easy to see lessons in simple gestures and deeds that were far more inscrutable when they actually occurred. What weight Mother's stories have taken on over the years. How carefully, and selectively, my memory has sifted all the experiences of my childhood. It's only natural to look for meaning in them, to look for the mold by which life has shaped you.

Some of the shaping forces and events stand out so clear and strong that I am tempted to point them out and make precise explanation of their influence on my life. This is probably a dangerous exercise, as likely to lead to misinterpretation as insight. I will resist that urge as much as possible and instead simply recount events and memories, and let them speak for themselves.

What remains in my memory from those early years are glimpses of family. Leon, my older brother by ten years, was Father's favorite. Father had a mind to groom him to come into the business. It would never happen, but he was the eldest and was obedient, so for a while he seemed inclined to go in that direction.

Misa, six years my senior, was the talented one in the family. He loved to draw. He would lie beneath the dining room table and sketch on a large pad. He wanted to be an architect, and did, in fact, create the plans for one of Father's houses.

Perhaps because he was nearer my own age, I was closest to Misa. Sometimes in the evening, he and I would gang up to wrestle with Leon. We'd roll around the floor in a great mock battle. Father, seated near by, would laugh. It's one of those events that lingers after all these years. It seems that it happened many times. The three boys wrestling, father laughing. A moment from the beginning of my life when everyone was there and happy, when the future stretched before us with great promise. But things change.

My parents were out of town when Misa took a hard fall while ice skating. He came home complaining of a headache, and the servants put him to bed. The next day he couldn't get out of bed. The doctor was summoned. My parents could not be reached. Misa's condition deteriorated and was finally determined to be meningitis.

He died the day my parents returned home. I was very young, 6 or 7, and do not remember the exact details of that tragic day, whether my parents saw him alive for the final moments. But I remember the resulting emotional devastation. Misa's death cast a pall over the household for many months.

In those earliest years, Elka was also a member of our family. She was much older than me, already a young adult when I was a boy. I thought she was my sister, but learned only years later, as I grew up, that she was really my aunt, a much younger sister of my mother. Mother raised her like her own child. Elka would go off to study medicine at the University of Bologna. She would marry a Jew, catch the last boat out of Italy before the fascists took control, and have a successful career as a pediatrician in Canada.

Then there was me. The youngest, indulged more than the others, I was more of a rascal. I loved to play in the barn behind our house, and enjoyed trips to the family farm outside of town. The cows and sheep were my pets. Father also dabbled in race horses, and I was especially fascinated by them. I would watch the grooms caring for them and putting them through their workouts. I loved their sleek, thoroughbred lines and their speed. Father kept them more for show than for any serious attempt at breeding racers, though there was a race course for trotters in Braila, and I dreamed of one day training a champion.

My mother much preferred that I learn the piano and concentrate on my studies. She had very definite ideas of proper conduct and the general direction that our lives should take. After a few halfhearted attempts at the keyboard, I surrendered that cultural pursuit to my brother Leon. I better satisfied Mother's expectations by being an avid reader.

Throughout my childhood I was a voracious reader. Books for me were what television would be for later generations of children. For hours every day I stayed glued to my books. Literature, science, history—I consumed it all. I haunted the used book shops in Braila, returning home with an armful of treasures.

Many books were in a foreign language. Any serious reader had to know French or German, since so many books had not been translated into Romanian. Large bookshelves were installed in my bedroom to hold my growing collection. I considered it a considerable mark of distinction to be living in a library.

Beyond intellectual development, Mother's governing principle for our behavior was that we should act like gentlemen, showing a great respect for adults, friends, and the opposite sex. Whenever I or one of my brothers violated these rules, we were all punished. Father had given Mother the instrument of discipline, a whip made of a certain bull organ, which hung on the wall as a constant reminder of the price of disobedience.

If one of us misbehaved, we were all lined up, bare bottoms exposed, and whipped. "This will teach you to watch out for each other," Mother would say, as she laid another stripe on our flesh. In the modern world this would pass for child abuse; in the world of my childhood it set the stern limits of proper behavior. We learned at an early age not to cross Mother. The steely force of her will stood at the gravitational center of our family. Even Father walked carefully in this area.

For me, as a child, there was the very strong sense of attachment, of being part of larger social units. Rules, expectations, and family history bound us to our immediate family. But we were also part of the much larger network of relatives and friends who would often gather at our house. Our home was jokingly called the "hotel," because of how often people visited or lodged with us.

My parents had come from the Bessarabian village of Arciz, a village so small that everyone was either a blood relative or felt bound by a form of village kinship. In our modern "global village," it's hard to understand the bonds that form among families who may have lived together in the same location for hundreds of years. Everyone knows everyone and knows everyone's business. More than that, they feel that they have a right, even a responsibility, to know such things.

Regularly throughout my childhood, we would pack up our trunks and ride the train to Arciz. We always stayed with Mother's family. Father's parents were a different sort, less warm and welcoming, and bad blood existed between them and my mother. Father's mother was not allowed in our house in Braila. This was my mother's ruling. No one ever spoke of the source of the conflict, but it was clear and adamant. Mother had a deep vindictive streak to her. She never forgave or forgot. Circumstances might force her to tolerate someone who had wronged her, but the injury would never heel. I'm afraid this same quality passed on to me.

My maternal grandparents worked very hard, were extremely frugal with their own needs, but generous with others. Grandfather ran a transportation business, using wagons and troikas to haul loads. In later years, when he drifted into mental illness, Grandmother operated the business on her own, with great success.

A visit to Arciz was a chance to reconnect with relatives and friends. A handful of cousins were always on hand as playmates. We milked the cows and took the horses down to the stream to wash them. Work was play for us when we had a group of other children. After the large mid-day meal, everyone took a nap, the children sprawling on the floor.

A broad main street ran through the center of Arciz. For the young it served as a promenade. Washed and dressed in their best clothes, they would parade up and down the street, observing each other. The etiquette of the ritual was that you could stop to talk with relatives but not with others. As I grew older and became more aware of girls, the promenade became a pleasant way to check out the opposite sex.

In my romantic imagination, I pictured my father as a boy strutting that same route, catching the eyes of the girls. He must have cut a very handsome figure, especially when he had grown to his full height of 6' 2". He would have been allowed to stop and talk with a certain, pretty, brown-haired girl, for she was his second cousin, Matilda Iutcovich. He stopped there often, talked at length, and finally lost his heart. This was the girl he married, a girl from the village, my mother.

Arciz was our home village, our family, our history, and even though we always returned to Braila, Arciz lodged in our hearts, along with the lives of those people and the values of that community.

It was that attachment that led villagers to our door in Braila. This one was on holiday and stopping to visit, this one had suffered a business setback and needed a loan. Aunts, uncles, and cousins added to the continual flow of guests. They were all welcomed. They brought news from Arciz, sometimes just the latest gossip of marriages and births. In the darkest days of political turmoil and war, they would be the only source of vital news of loved ones.

Father, who could be very tough in his business dealings, was generous with friends. He took people in and loaned them money, never expecting its return. When we had a house full of guests, we often entertained them at a local restaurant called Dino's, famous for their stuffed veal head. Food would overflow the tables. Wine would be served from the barrel father kept on reserve there.

When the feasting drew to a close, the women returned home and the men stayed on to drink. Father was not an alcoholic, but given the occasion, he was a prodigious drinker, and evenings at Dino's, with good fellowship, were the right occasion. One of his good friends was a wealthy Greek merchant. They often passed an evening together at Dino's, a mammoth bottle of wine between them. The evening ended when the bottle had been drained.

Traditions of the village and its network of relationships helped to forge Father's outlook on life, even as practical experience schooled him on how to succeed in business. The unique quality that he brought to his career was that he thought big and took chances. Early business success during World War I nurtured that quality, but it was such an integral part of his personality that it motivated all his dealings.

There was an energy, a momentum, that pushed him along his career. Hurdles meant nothing, setback were meaningless—they were part of the game. Keep moving, keep working, another deal waited around the corner. Accumulating money was not a final goal for him. Money was simply the inevitable result of the big deal, the successful operation, of the job well done.

I always had money, and I sometimes spent it lavishly or foolishly. He rarely complained. And when he did, it was generally because I had some how disobeyed him, or had treated someone in a manner he considered inappropriate. This code of conduct, of trust and respect, lay at the foundation of a good life.

Not that he had romantic expectations of others. "As long as you have money and a full table, you have friends," he often told me. During the troublesome times of the War and the political change that followed, when the polite traditions governing social and business interaction changed or disappeared, only money made things happen and insured survival.

But in more civil times, the codes of business were well-established. You dealt fairly with everyone and expected the same in return. A handshake was as good as a written contract. To make the wheels turn smoothly, you cultivated a large circle of associates for whom you were generous with favors, because the day always came when you too would need a favor, and would rely upon those associates to be equally generous with you.

To see Father's darker side you only had to violate that code. After his cattle export fiasco, when he was broke, he went to the local bank for a loan. The banker was unwilling to loan him money, which enraged Father. "One day I will buy this bank and fire you!" Father shouted at the banker. It was not an idle flash of temper. Not too many years down the road, when Father was once again successful, he made a point to purchase that bank and fire the banker.

* * *

In 1937, my parents announced that I would be sent away to boarding school in Bucharest. It came as a surprise, a shock really, since neither of my brothers had attended boarding school. My brother Leon was set to enter a university in Czechoslovakia that same year, but that was different.

I was only eight years old. I was doing well at the Catholic primary school I attended. All of my friends attended there. Even my Jewish friends, Silviu and Ion attended, wearing the same black, choir-boy smock and eagerly collecting the picture cards of Bible scenes and saints that the nuns gave us for learning our lessons.

I had my routines, my friends, the warm embrace of family. How could I survive without those things? I remember being very sad at this turn of events and dreading the approaching day of my departure. Bucharest was about 160 kilometers away, but it might have been China for how large the distance loomed in my imagination.

Most of all, I did not want to leave my mother. She called me her baby and said that I was "her purse," a wonderful metaphor for how treasured was our relationship. But I had no doubt that the decision to send me away was her decision. She was the one who so highly valued education. She, too, was the one to prize discipline and order, things she had sometimes found lacking in my character. Perhaps she wanted me to acquire those traits. Perhaps she thought that a boarding school would provide the best possible education and that a good education was worth the pain of separation.

I did not know her reasons. She did not explain her decisions to me. And, of course, I did not argue or ask for an explanation. That would have been the height of impudence. The wishes of my mother were as unchallengeable as the forces of nature, and the consequences of opposing them could be as dire.

When my brother Leon had graduated from high school that spring, he announced to Mother that he planned to marry his girlfriend. Oh, the fire in her eyes when she heard that. I can still see her face as she descended the stairway and paused at the bottom, dark and ominous as a thunder cloud.

"Come here," she said to Leon, gesturing with her finger, and he shuffled closer. Whereupon she hit him so hard aside the head that a tooth came out. "Do you want to get married?" she asked.

"No," came his choked reply.

"Good," she said, and only then gave a tight smile to approve his good sense. The world had been put right, order restored. He would need to acquire education first and find employment. Then, and only then, so frail and foolish a flower as romance might have its time to bloom.

Mother and Father were both supportive and cautious about my youthful romances, perhaps because my romances never threatened to take so dramatic a turn as marriage.

Father took me to Bucharest. It was a sixteen hour journey on a train that stopped at every town and village along the way. Each mile, slipping by with agonizing slowness, heightened my anxiety to be traveling so far from home for the first time. Each mile took me closer to a new life that I would have to face on my own. I longed for words of comfort from my father. The moment felt important to me. I wondered what he was thinking. But not many words passed between us on that trip.

Father was a tall, solidly-built man with dark features. His family was descended from "free peasants," a distinction from peasants who were feudally bound to a landowner, and a source of some pride. His father had not attended school at all. He, himself, had done quite well with only a high school education. Life had been his classroom. But above all else, he valued the sacred bond of family. If he was sad at my being away from home, perhaps it was balanced by an appreciation for the progression in educational achievement. He, Joseph Iutcovich, son of a peasant, was sending his own son off to a private boarding school in the capital.

In Bucharest, Father delivered me to my dormitory, and it seemed a barren and joyless place compared to home. "Work hard and do well," he said as he surrendered me to this new phase of my life. Then he admonished me to make my parents proud. This was a recurring theme in the Lessons of Life—make your parents proud.

That first night, I looked from the dormitory window onto the grey expanse of Bucharest and felt terribly alone.

I had arrived in the city where I would spend the majority of my life for the next two decades. There would be times when I would feel at home in this city, as an adolescent and university student finding his place in the world. But, there would be other times when there was no place for me in Bucharest, when I would violate the expectations of my family, friends, or government. There would be other times, as well, and these were the most troubling, when the expectations I had of the world, or of myself, would blur and lose meaning, and every decision confronting me seemed weighted with life-altering significance.

But on this night, my first in Bucharest, my first on my own, I was a frightened boy. Still, nothing seemed more important to me on that fall evening in 1937 then to honor my father's advice to make my parents proud. I vowed to do just that.

2
War Comes to Romania

The regimen was very structured at boarding school, the discipline strict, which wasn't to my liking. Awake at 6 a.m., classes from 7 until 4. Many of the teachers were university professors, and they did not hesitate to pile on the work: Latin, foreign languages, classics of Romanian and western literature, the sciences. King Carol's dour portrait stared down at us from the walls of the classrooms, as though he too had expectations of us. After all, this was a private academy in the capitol city of our great country. Our academic records were strong enough to get us here, and our parents could afford to send us. High expectations were justified.

For a long time, I was sick with worry that I would be unable to meet the school's high standards. I feared failure. If I failed, I would never again be able to face my parents or my friends back home. My life would be ruined. If I did not score well on a test, I doubled my efforts, driven by this new credo that had taken hold of me for this first great endeavor of my young life, namely that defeat was unacceptable. I would survive, I would do well, I would make my parents proud.

Most nights we studied in the library until 10 p.m., then later in our rooms, if the demands of homework required it. They often did. I did it unflinchingly, slowly overcoming my initial anxiety, motivated by my father's admonition, my mother's iron will, and my reverence for and fear of my teachers.

I remember being very focused on my studies. Especially in those early years, I led a rather monkish existence.

But those years were also my introduction to Bucharest. The size and grandeur of the city made a strong impression on me. Because of its lively culture and its palaces, its wide, tree-lined avenues and spacious parks, Bucharest was known as the "Paris of the Balkans." Romania was a flourishing country, with one of the leading economies in Europe, and here I was in the heart of things.

My dawning awareness of the larger world also began to take in the political change heavy in the air in the late 1930s. Nazism had come of age in Germany, and Romania had its own, home-grown Nazis—the Iron Guard. Like fascists in Germany, like fascists then and today, the Iron Guard gathered support among social misfits, the dissatisfied, and the alienated by promising to rejuvenate the country. They would lead a moral crusade against all those who were betrayers of Romania's historic legacy of greatness. This simplistic message played well during those economic hard times and gained a large following.

Leading the Iron Guard's list of betrayers of Romania were the Jews, followed by Communists, then the capitalists, who exploited the peasants. Members of the Iron Guard looked rather smart in their green uniform shirts. I would see them on the street and in public places. They carried an air of arrogance about them, as though they knew a secret that the rest of us did not.

One day while walking near school, I saw two Green Shirts yelling at a man, shoving him against a building. Punches to the stomach doubled him up and one to the face dropped him to the ground. This was not done as some street crime but quite openly, as though it was their right or an honorable thing for public viewing. I hurried on by.

A few years earlier, the Iron Guard had assassinated two national politicians, the noted historian and former prime minister Nicolae Iorga and the well respected Prime Minister Ion Duca. Duca had tried to uphold law and maintain the parliament. He had represented Romania's best hope for normalcy during a time of economic crisis and political turmoil. His Iron Guard murderers were later acquitted by a military tribunal.

King Carol tried to repress the Iron Guard, but their cause was too broadly embraced by certain elements of the population, and of course, supported by Germany's Nazis. It would gall me immensely in later years to see some of the intellectuals who had supported the Iron Guard, try to distance themselves from its excesses and failures. One in particular who comes to mind is the renowned religious historian, Mircea Eliade, who was an early supporter of the Iron Guard and never disavowed their cause. His friend and colleague, Nae Ionescu, was considered the ideologist for the Iron Guard. Eliade never condemned him nor broke ranks with him.

After the war, Eliade would receive academic appointments at prestigious universities in Europe and the U.S. People didn't know or care about his past. America, and its universities, were very accommodating to old Nazis who could make themselves useful. So, Eliade's past did not raise an eyebrow.

Of course, so much would come to light after the war about how people and governments conducted themselves, especially in regard to the Holocaust. It revealed most shockingly that anti-semitism was not the sole province of the Nazis, but was pervasive in the West, and that it extended to the U.S. State Department and even to the conduct of Pope Pius the XII.

Perhaps it was inevitable, from the time of those assassinations on, that Romania would drift towards fascism and Nazism. I had arrived in Bucharest four years after those tragic events, at a time when the Iron Guard was becoming increasingly open, influential, and dangerous.

Instinctively, I did not share the news of what I saw on the streets with my classmates, but kept it to myself. I remember the event now simply as some unpleasantness I witnessed, not as a landmark in my awareness of approaching fascism.

And yet, in hindsight, that period seemed to mark a shift in my outlook towards life and in the national outlook, as well. We were entering a period in which we would live a dual life. A rift was beginning to form between what we thought and what we said, between the larger public world and the shrinking private world. But it was so small an event on this occasion as to barely register on my awareness.

The focus of my life continued to be Braila, and an idyllic childhood. Holidays and summer vacations at home stand out more in my memory than the longer months of isolation in Bucharest. In the early years, Father would come by train to take me home, and I would be so proud to report that I had scored well on some test or paper. Before long I rode the train back to Braila by myself, back to my home, back to family and friends, back to my comfortable nest on the 3rd floor of our house.

Smells of breakfast would rouse me in the morning, and I would make it downstairs in time to see Father off on his daily cattle-buying excursions. He would wrap a large money belt around his middle. The chauffeur would fire up the old Fiat, father would climb in back, and off he would go. My brother Leon, who was studying textile engineering at the university, had lost all interest in learning about cattle dealing. He was a young man now, and had his own interests and friends. As did I.

Silviu, Ion, Dietrich, Emil, my classmates from primary school, were still my closest friends. We had all the usual childhood adventures. In summer we often swam in the Danube. I was forbidden from having a boat but dreamed of cruising up and down that grand river.

One summer, this boating fantasy took such a compelling grip on Silviu and me that we secretly purchased a small sail boat. We named it "The She" and would sneak down to the river as often as possible for sailing excursions. What exhilarating adolescent freedom to be sailing to adventure in our tiny craft. Until our secret began to unwind.

"Where are all my bed sheets going?" my mother complained loudly to the servants. She thought they were stealing them, when in fact, I had made off with them to make a sail for our boat. My father eventually learned of our escapade and put an abrupt end to my nautical career. This was one of the first times that I directly went against my parents' rules. I was learning that sometimes the temptation to disobey my parents was very great indeed.

So much of my time in these years was spent on the family farm, just a few miles outside Braila. It was a playground, bustling with distractions. There were buildings to explore, fields to roam, horses to ride, wistful days to spend tending the sheep. I had to watch each activity: milking, planting, harvesting, shearing of the sheep, grinding of grain at the mill. There was no end of things to excite a young boy.

One day a new car showed up in our driveway—a Chevrolet. Father had purchased it second-hand from a local dentist. It was larger and more powerful than the Fiat. At Father's direction, the engine was overhauled and the interior reupholstered. Father was proud to be driven around in his new vehicle. It lent him a greater air of importance when he traveled to cattle markets and allowed him to cover more territory. Cars were wonderful, I conceded, but I still preferred horses.

Each year, as summer drew to a close, I would suffer a mood of dejection at the thought of leaving family and friends. But September would come, and once more I rode the train back to my other life as a student on my own in the big city. Back again to Bucharest, where the world seemed to push with mounting insistence into my sphere of existence.

It may seem strange, but I can't recall the exact details of the first time I encountered a dead body on the street. Perhaps it was on the way home from a play, perhaps it was a dark form glimpsed in an alleyway. Neither could I say how many times I witnessed Green Shirts beating up someone on the streets. But these things began to happen with increasing frequency as the clouds of war gathered on the horizon. And as they became a more common presence, they ceased to have the same shock value.

In the fall of 1939, the bodies of some Iron Guard members were displayed in the public squares of some cities, with this inscription, "This is the punishment for traitors to the people and the country." They had been executed by

King Carol in what had become a series of reprisal killings between the government and the Iron Guard.

But a few dead Iron Guard did not stop the tide of history. The world was changing. Huge political events brooded just outside my narrowly-defined world. A growing mood of anxiety crept into the safe world of my school. Discussions of current events touched on the activities of Germany and the brewing diplomatic and military storm heading towards conflict.

In 1940, I no sooner arrived home on summer vacation than two dramatic pieces of news broke. One: the Soviet Union seized Bessarabia. This inflamed passions throughout Romania. Once more Romania had been assaulted by its old enemy Russia. Once more Bessarabia had passed to Russian control.

Great anxiety reigned in our home. We feared for the well being of our relatives. We urged them to come to Braila to live with us. Mother pleaded with her mother, but Grandmother could be stubborn as a tree. She had lived through other wars. She had lived under Russian control before. She would not be alarmed by this shift in the political wind.

But other shifts in the political wind also screamed for attention. That same month, when Paris fell to the German Army, the desperateness of our circumstances became clear. We seemed to live on the edge that summer. All of Europe was choosing up sides in the war, and yet King Carol kept Romania uncommitted, as though neutrality would hold evil at bay and keep us safe for a few more months or weeks.

But the Nazi poison crept deeper into Romania, coming ever closer to our lives. One hot summer day, my Jewish friend Silviu and I were walking through the alleyways of Braila, headed for our favorite swimming spot along the Danube, when four boys began following us.

"Jidan," they yelled. The word twisted with vicious hate in their mouths. Perhaps the closest English equivalent would be "kike," or "nigger." It was a common, anti-semitic insult.

"Go back to Palestine where you belong," they shouted, as we quickened our pace.

They followed, continuing their taunts, pushing closer, eager for a fight. Silviu and I tore wooden slats from a picket fence and defended ourselves, like swordsmen fighting barbarians. We came out on top of that scrap, but it didn't take too many such encounters to sober you to the possibility of violence, to yourself and those you cared for.

The vicious anti-semitism of the Green Shirts became a growing concern for Romania's Jews. My friend Dietrich was German of Jewish origin. His family left the country for Argentina. Many Jews fled to the Soviet Union, reasoning that their chances of survival were better there than under a fascist government. The families of my friends Ion and Silviu chose to stay on. Although my family was not Jewish, there were Jews in the family. My father's sisters had both married Jews. And, of course, many of our closest friends were Jewish.

Throughout this period, tension rose to a palpable level in my family. There was already talk that the Iron Guard wanted to confiscate Father's business. Because he was a capitalist? Because of Jews in the family? Who knew. What did it matter *why*? Would it happen? What would we do then? Would harm come to the family? Throughout the war, fear for the safety and welfare of the family was never far from our minds.

Except with family and very close friends, you did not talk about these things. But among that close circle, you exchanged your latest experience or the latest rumor—a store ransacked, a Jew losing his job, someone disappearing, bodies found. Sometimes the stories seemed too nightmarish to be true, but too often they were.

From Father's large circle of friends and business associates, he heard many horror stories. In the intimacy of our evening meal, he would tell us, "They burned down the house of a Jew in Tulcea." He would be frustrated or angry about such behavior and rail against the Iron Guard.

But the stories became steadily more frightening. "They found bodies in a slaughter house in Bucharest, Jews hung up on hooks like sides of beef." I remember vividly to this day when he told us that, and it still evokes the same horrific image of slaughter. Father looked at Mother gravely. She went to speak but caught herself.

I think Mother wanted to dismiss it as rumor, an obvious fabrication; it was simply too horrendous. That was your first line of defense. The accounts, or rumors, of such heinous events were threatening. Each one made you feel just a little bit more vulnerable. If it could happen in Bucharest, in Tulcea, or in the next block, then it could happen to our family as well. So, you wanted to find some reason not to believe such stories.

I could see in Mother's eyes on that occasion that she wanted desperately to dismiss what she was hearing. But excuses and denials could no longer hide the truth. There was a long silence at our dinner table. There seemed no clearer indication at the time that our country was plunging into an abyss. How should one react? How could one keep harm away?

"Be careful," my parents warned me when they sent me back to Bucharest that fall. It was the only armor they could give against this evil. I took it to mean, "Don't speak of these things," and "Don't draw attention to yourself."

I knew from the conversations of my school mates that many of them came from wealthy families that shared the Iron Guard's anti-semitic views. So, if I saw Iron Guard members, in their distinctive green shirts, vandalizing a store or beating someone, I did not mention it to anyone. If I encountered a body on the street, I did not show revulsion or too keen an interest. I averted my gaze. I did not share it with my schoolmates. I kept everything to myself.

Even an idle remark on my part to a classmate might be reported to the authorities. Perhaps Iutcovich had sympathy for these criminals, they might think. Perhaps he doubted the appropriateness of the Iron Guard's methods or the legitimacy of their cause. Let us look more closely at Iutcovich's background.

In a way, I wanted to be as invisible as the crimes I refused to see. Otherwise, I might be expelled from school, or beaten, or there might be consequences for my family. So, I was careful, as my parents had advised. I made no close friends at boarding school and attended to my studies.

Then, things began to happen quickly. Increasing pressure from Germany forced King Carol to abdicate to his son, Michael, allowing the fascists to take control of the government in the person of General Ion Antonescu. The Iron Guard was not a part of the government, but they maintained an unofficial, underground existence and continued with their program of violence.

Antonescu installed a military government committed to regaining Bessarabia from the Soviet Union. This put it in league with the Nazis. German soldiers began appearing on the streets of Bucharest. As the end of the school year approached the following spring, full scale preparations were under way for a joint Romanian-German invasion of Russia.

I was eager to be home in this time of crisis. I knew that my parents were very worried about family still living in Bessarabia. War was poised to sweep over them. Arciz would no longer be safe. Even our stubborn, old grandmother would have to accept that.

Soldiers crowded the train to Braila on my trip home. It seemed by the congestion on the roads that much of the German army still relied on horses. They pulled a continuing caravan of wagons and artillery pieces towards the east. Braila buzzed with military activity. It made me worry whether Braila itself would be safe.

When I got home I found that the German army was there as well. A Nazi officer was being quartered in our house. He had been given a room on the second floor and took some of his meals with us. He was very courteous, and his family in Germany sounded very much like our own. Still, I resented this intrusion into the family, especially when the officer shared our traditional family meal time in the evening. We could not talk freely, nor share the trivial things of our day, without an awkward self-consciousness. Everyone must do their part for the war effort, we had been told.

Meanwhile, this huge war machine gathered on the Romanian border poised to strike at Russia. Mother was frantic about the safety of family in Arciz, especially Grandmother. There were no longer any communications with Bessarabia. Mother assured us, and herself, that the people of Arciz would be well aware of the coming invasion. They would flee *en masse* long before fighting broke out. Even stubborn old women would know enough to leave.

In June of 1941 Germany launched a three-pronged attack against the Soviet Union, a northern assault through the Baltic States and a central push directly towards Moscow. The southern assault, under General von Rundstedt, struck through southern Poland towards the Ukraine, the Crimea, and the Black Sea. The combined armies of Germany and Romania quickly overran Bessarabia, and the war swept away from our borders. There was no word on our family, but we held to the faith that they were safe, deep in the vast interior of Russia, where the fighting would never reach.

I turned twelve that year, and to say that life went on as usual would be a gross misrepresentation. Because we were scared. All around us, for the next few years, the most extraordinary events were occurring, tangling our lives in tragedy and intrigue.

Still, a semblance of normalcy prevailed. Father carried on business as usual. I suspect my father felt somewhat protected by his position in society. He had no political affiliation, he was a successful businessman, he had a network of influential friends and associates, and he had money. Romania was a country where money could buy you out of most trouble.

One of his friends, a high-ranking military officer, told him not to worry. Romania was trying to build up its industry and agriculture to support the war. Even more cattle than before would be needed. Business would be good. His friend was right.

"Why don't you come with me," Father said to me one day as he prepared for another cattle-buying trip. I readily agreed, and joined him on the first of what would become our regular schedule of such trips together.

I felt so wonderfully important, settled into the plush rear seat of the Chevrolet with Father as Nicu drove us into the countryside. We often traveled to the small towns west of Braila, along Father's regular routes. These towns had marketplaces where people gathered to sell produce and livestock. We would find some farmer sitting on his wagon, a steer that he wished to sell tethered behind.

Father had a keen eye for livestock and could usually judge their weight within a few kilos. When a farmer showed him an animal he wished to sell, Father looked it over carefully, then the bargaining commenced. Father would grasp the farmer's hand and shake it, sometimes vigorously, during the entire negotiations. When the deal was struck, Father paid him in cash, and we'd be off to the next farmer with an animal, then on to the next market town.

Sometimes, as we drove the roads, I saw a herd of animals being led across country on a cattle drive, as farmers drove them to the government-run slaughter houses or to the big market towns, such as Tecuci and Birlad. During the big livestock markets, these towns came alive with activity, a cross between an agricultural fair and a carnival, great diversion for a young boy.

There seemed to be a smooth order to life in the countryside that I found appealing. War raged across the continent, the world. Europe had struck the course of self destruction. Yet these hard-working farmers continued to plant their crops, tend their animals, and worry about the weather, as they had for millennia. There was something inexpressibly profound in this devotion to a cause higher than war and politics.

I enjoyed these excursions with Father. They would continue throughout the war when I was home, and even into the post-war years when I was on break from the university. They brought us closer and taught me a few things about running a business and striking a deal. Father always dealt fairly with the farmers. They knew that and respected him. But he also knew the market and was able to turn a tidy profit from his dealings.

But, of course, whenever we returned from the markets, the war always waited to greet us. We followed the progress of the war through the Nazi-controlled media and foreign radio broadcasts. Von Rundstedt's army swept quickly past Lvov and Kiev. Romanian troops captured Odessa. Soon German forces were on the outskirts of Leningrad and attacking Smolensk. It appeared as though the vaunted German *blitzkrieg* would achieve victory in the East as quickly as it had in the West.

"I just received my official notice." Silviu showed up at my house one day with bad news. "They're sending me to a camp. Ion, too." He wore a brave front, but I could tell he was frightened. Jews in Romania did not have to wear the star of David, and Romania did not have the same officially organized extermination program as did the Nazis. Still, there were massacres and internment camps, and Jews suffered many abuses at the hands of our own Nazis, the Iron Guard.

The day of Silviu's departure was close at hand, and with a shrug of the shoulders he signaled his resolve to go. "It will be like prison; they will work us hard, but maybe it will be a safe place to ride out the war." I shrugged, too, not knowing what to say.

Only after he had been transported, did we learn that he had not gone to a Romanian camp. Ion had, but Silviu was sent to Treblinka. Why Silviu had been selected, we did not know, but we understood that he would likely not survive. Father resolved to do something about it and began making inquiries.

On this occasion, and on many others, I would see the power of Father's connections. Over the years he had developed a network of friendships, business connections, and private contacts. He routinely gave gifts to important people. At Christmas, for instance, he would ship off casks of feta cheese or smoked hams to politicians and army officers. He would invite them to lavish dinners at local restaurants. He knew that the smooth operation of any business depended on the good will of those people who controlled the apparatus of government.

"As long as you have money and a full table, you have friends," he would repeat this wisdom to me. Of course, in later years, when the times became even more difficult, the "gifts" became increasingly large. Until, eventually, no offering was large enough to keep harm from our door.

We continued to have a succession of German officers quartered in our home. Like many Romanians we harbored mixed feelings about the war. Officially, the Nazis were our allies, and yet we hated everything they represented, and hated as well the fascist character of our own government.

Certain tableaus from the past tend to linger in my mind because they were so striking, and this period furnished me with many such scenes. In one, my family is seated in our living room as the sweet strains of a Mozart concerto dance in the air. Crisp, delicate notes of a piano hold us entranced. The source of such beauty? A young, German officer playing our piano. Imagine that, I thought, a soldier playing Mozart, a *Nazi* playing Mozart.

Like most of the other officers who shared our home, he was handsome, polite, and cultured. It struck me on this occasion that this was the type of well-mannered, well-educated "gentlemen" that Mother had always wanted me to be. It challenged my adolescent understanding to fit this character into the behavior of the Nazis.

"If you are so cultured, why do you do such terrible things?" I asked him later in the evening, embarrassing my parents. It was an easy question for him, requiring no thought. "Orders," he said.

My father operated at the same basic level of unquestioning action. Except that his impulses were humanitarian. Throughout his life, he felt a genuine obligation to help others. I don't know what behind-the-scenes maneuvering Father did for Silviu, but large sums of money went into the right pockets. Eventually we got word that Silviu had been transferred from Treblinka to a Romanian camp.

Before long, Silviu learned that if he paid a little money to the guards at the camp, they would allow him to visit home on weekends. His prediction was coming true—With a little help from Father, Silviu would get to ride out the war in the safety of the camp.

But the war was far from over. Nazi radio broadcasts glorified the victories of the German offensive in the Soviet Union. Their armies captured 300,000 Red Army prisoners in July, in August another 300,000 at Smolensk and 100,000 at Uman, then 600,000 in the Ukraine that September.

However, as we learned to read the subtle, between-the-lines reality coloring the propaganda, we realized that battling Russia would not be the same as battling Poland or France. Capture three Soviet armies, and what had Germany accomplished? Annihilate a few more Soviet armies and they were no better off. They still could not claim victory, because there were other Soviet armies waiting to do battle. This war would not end soon.

As the war dragged on, we longed for news about our relatives from Arciz. Occasionally, someone from the village would find his or her way to our house in Braila with news. Mother always asked about her mother. We eventually learned that many of the villagers had left in panic, fleeing by train before the German advance. But we discovered nothing about Grandmother's fate. This painful waiting would continue for years, even after the war, until my mother finally met up with a woman who had taken that same fateful train ride.

My grandmother had been on board the train, making the dash for safety along with others, the woman told her. However, at one of the stops, she got off the train to look for food, the woman said. And when the train started moving again, she had not returned. Grandmother never made it back on the train. That was all the friend knew.

Mother was anguished but still clung to a small hope that her mother had survived. If war was a force of nature that rolled without conscience over individual lives, it was also capricious in whom it spared. Those given up for lost could suddenly appear, bob up like a cork from the flood of events. It could happen, but it didn't. As was more often the case in war, Grandmother simply disappeared. We never heard another word on her fate. We were left with just that one last image of her, hungry, standing alone in some nameless rail station, watching the train depart without her.

3
Life Goes On

In the handful of photographs that have survived from this time, there is one of me at the family farm, reclining on the ground, surrounded by sheep. Somewhere in my mid-teens, I look like a roguish shepherd, tall and thin, with an easy smile. I look quite carefree, yet almost a man. I can't recall who stood behind the lens on that occasion, a childhood friend or the woman who had become my lover.

The fellow in that photograph occupies that cusp of tranquility during the war. The halcyon days of childhood had not yet totally surrendered to war or politics. The full weight of adult concerns had not yet descended upon his shoulders.

Maybe it is a trick of memory, viewing one's childhood through the lens of half a century, but the ordinary events of my growing up seem vested with special significance. As though they had a role to fulfill. As though I had to live them more deeply, or cling to them more tightly, to convince myself life could be ordinary and secure with war all around.

The war years were a time of coming of age for me, a weave of historical events and adolescent landmarks, when passions of every sort gripped me with great intensity. I was 12 years old when the war began and 16 when it ended, a schoolboy intellectual, already used to living on my own and fending for myself.

In 1941, the year Romania entered the war, I bought a book on the philosophy of Spinoza. I studied it very carefully, not understanding one word. But I knew it was an important book, filled with wisdom and I ached to know its mysteries. I carried it around, just to be seen with it, just to let others wonder about so tender a youth reading philosophy.

As later generations of youngsters would make heros of athletes, I admired writers. I wanted to read them, talk about them, and be like them. Writers of many subjects and many nations filled my shelves. For pure entertainment, nothing could beat the action-adventure stories of Alexander Dumas. *The Three Musketeers,* and *The Count of Monte Cristo* were special favorites, as was the science fiction of Jules Verne.

Intellectuals were my role models. I remember a certain Professor Zahn, a Romanian sociologist. I had read several of his books and been impressed, both by the Professor and this science called sociology that studied peoples' behavior. Professors enjoyed a very exalted position in Romanian society and Zahn was one of the best. Years later, I would be shocked and disgusted to learn that Zahn had become a fascist. How could it be that one who seemed so admirable had evil in his character? It dealt a profound jolt to my innocence and taught a valuable lesson about the blind adulation of a role model.

However, when I was young, I had no such delusions. Zahn's star shone bright for me. I admired him greatly and fantasized about being a famous professor.

Heaven for me was a visit to one of the used book shops in Braila. I recall that musty, dusty smell of used books, the shadowy labyrinth of tall shelves, and row upon row, the spines inscribed in Romanian, German or French, the books inviting me to sample their knowledge or thrill to their adventure. "What will we do with all these books?" Mother would grumble good-naturedly when I'd cart home another armful to add to the stacks in my bedroom.

It was at one of the book stores that I met a man I came to know simply as Bebu. He was middle-aged, unemployed, and supported entirely by his aunts, with whom he lived. Lazy, some might call him, but he was the closest thing to a pure intellectual that I have ever met. Without a career or a marriage, content with a "life of the mind," he engaged in few activities that brought him in contact with others.

That may explain the relationship that formed between us. He felt a bond with another habitué of the dusty world of second-hand book shops. I was hungry to learn of life through literature and philosophy. Bebu delighted in sharing what he had read, but was equally thrilled to feast at the same table with me on a banquet of fine books.

From casual conversations in the book shops, our relationship went to the loaning of books. Bebu had a huge library. I had only to mention an author or title, and the chances are he had it, or one like it, or one influenced by it, or another work by the same author. I would visit his aunts' house to watch as Bebu selected a few books from his shelves that he thought would please me or that I should read, and I would go home with one or three or five volumes to eagerly devour.

With Bebu I could not *pretend* to have read a book, because he always had questions. How well did I think this character was motivated? Wasn't the plot twist similar to the Tolstoy book he had loaned me the previous month? We had rousing debates about such things when he began to visit me at home.

Initially, my mother was suspicious of these visits, of the whole relationship. Why was this older man so interested in her adolescent son? What did they do for so long in Mark's room? On one occasion—Mother later confessed—she even peered through the keyhole of my room to assure that nothing unwholesome was going on. Once Mother knew that Bebu had no evil intentions, she welcomed him warmly, and he became a regular visitor in our home.

The more devious intentions of corrupting my character fell to my brother Leon. In the fall of 1941 he and a friend paid me an unexpected visit at boarding school. "Come, little brother, we have a surprise for you." I had no idea what they were up to, but they laughed as though it were a trick. Only after we were out on the street did Leon say, "Today you will be a man." I was only 12; the prospect of being a man pleased me. Then he explained that they were taking me to visit a prostitute. He and his friend laughed again, and I went cold inside.

Prostitution was not only legal in Romania, but was a well-established institution. The houses were licensed and the prostitutes regularly examined by doctors. Young men typically acquired their sexual education at the hands of such professionals. Every town of any size had its "house" or district for such trade. Leon led me to Bucharest's red-light district.

I, of course, had no experience in these matters. Leon, a 22-year-old university graduate and man of the world, was a whore house veteran. I shook with nerves as they led me into the house. How was one to behave in a whore house? What did one do with a woman? What if I could not do what was expected?

We entered a living room of the house, where several women sat about. Leon made the selection for me, an attractive brown-haired woman in her early 20s. She looked so normal; she might have been the sister or aunt of one of my friends. That put me somewhat at ease. She led me to an upstairs bedroom.

I sat self-consciously on the edge of the bed, while she casually removed her dress, then her undergarments. My heart galloped faster than a race horse, as she urged me off the bed, undressed me, then introduced me to the pleasures of the flesh.

Her name was Maria, I learned, and she was so patient and understanding, so accomplished a teacher, that I regularly returned to visit her on my own for additional instruction. I became as diligent a student in her classroom as I was at school. The price of instruction was 20 leis, about $1, per visit.

Of course, it was a time of the double standard. Men were allowed, even expected to be sexually experienced and women were expected to be virgins. There were exceptions, of course, but at least when it came to marriage, most men would not have considered taking a wife who was not a virgin. Yet they employed every artifice to get women to bed. Thus, the usefulness of prostitution in such a society—an outlet for the sexual urge, a bulwark for the institution of virginity.

Now I had something to look forward to in Bucharest. Whenever I wished, I could leave the regimented world of school, where I was a mere boy, for that other part of Bucharest, for Maria's house, and be received as a man. I would never go with any of the other women, only Maria. I savored the easy familiarity we enjoyed. I had learned small things about her personality and background, enough to make our visits more personal. Sometimes, I would tip her handsomely or give her some small gift.

In the rush of adolescent hormones, I formed a genuine affection for her. I'm sure it was nothing more than a pleasant business relationship for her, but I took it for love. What I didn't yet understand was that while she had much to teach me about sex, my education in love had to wait for another occasion.

Love knocked on my door for the first time in the person of a girl named Phylicia. I was about 15, on a double date with my friend Emil. "She has a boyfriend, but he's in prison," Emil had told me. Phylicia was an attractive girl, from a good family. We talked easily, laughed, and had fun. I was smitten. I wanted that evening to last forever. However, as with all my social outings in Braila, I had to keep a close eye on the clock and end things about 8:30 p.m.

Regardless of whom I dated or where I went, I had to be home by 9 p.m. That was the hour of our family dinner, the one time during the day when everyone had to sit down together. Today we would call it "quality time." This was not just an appointment one tried to keep, it was a sacred commitment. Missing the family dinner was a slap in my parents' face, a slap at the family. Few things roused their ire more than missing this ritual. So, I tore myself from Phylicia, from what I knew would be the one and only true love of my life, to race home and be with my family.

Like so many first loves, mine for Phylicia consumed me. I wanted to be with her all of the time, do things for her, impress her. One day as we strolled the streets of Braila, we stopped to admire a coat in a store window.

"It's Astrakhan," Phylicia cooed, in a melting tone of voice. "Isn't it beautiful?"

"Let's go in and try it on," I suggested. She looked incredulous, but I urged her on.

Inside, she slipped into the coat, caressed the sleeve, and hugged it around her. Astrakhan is made from the pelts of very young lambs. The fleece is black, tightly curled, and exquisitely soft. My mother owned an Astrakhan coat. Phylicia looked beautiful in it.

"It was made for you," I said, and then called over the shop keeper and told him I wished to purchase it. The coat was an enormously expensive luxury, much like a mink coat might have been elsewhere in the world. "Charge it to my father," I told the shop keeper.

It was a grand gesture that very much impressed Phylicia. Of course, I had to brace myself for the consequences of my impulsiveness. I happened to be upstairs the day my father arrived home in a foul mood, having received the charges from the shop. "Do you know what your son has done?" he shouted to my mother. The edge on his voice made me cringe. I always knew I was in trouble when he gave ownership of me over to Mother—*your* son. I made a quick mental survey of the possible punishments that might befall me, then cocked my ear to follow the conversation.

After Father's heated explanation of the circumstances, Mother said, "Didn't you teach him to be a gentleman?" Just that. So simple an interpretation. I must have held my breath for several minutes, but Father had no reply. Neither he nor Mother ever mentioned a word to me of the incident.

The notion of "gentleman" has lost most of its meaning today, but for my mother it denoted an attitude towards one's role in the world, defining not only how one would behave but also what one would value.

As for Phylicia? Our relationship sailed blissfully along for about a year and a half, until her former boyfriend was released from prison. She left me for him and broke my heart. She also kept the coat.

*   *   *

Our farm always bustled with activity, especially in summer when I returned home from school. I'd ride a horse the few kilometers from town to spend the day, or several days, in the country. A Greek named Stefan ran the farm for us. His wife, Katty, had the most dark, soulful eyes that oozed sensuality. I would sometimes take meals with them, but would stay in the main house by myself.

Though Father made the major decisions regarding farm operations, he seldom visited there. From my early teenage years on, he gave me increasing responsibility for managing operations, and I became fully involved in the day-to-day management of the farm, learning from our overseer and from experience about running such a large enterprise.

We had purchased a two-year-old race horse that I named Danak. Few things were as thrilling as riding in my jaunty, two-wheeled carriage, urging Danak to break-neck speed on the road to Braila. On several occasions, I ran into the same fellow in an automobile. I'd pull along side him, then nose ahead. He'd speed up, and soon we'd be racing. The automobile would kick up clouds of dust. Danak would fly, bouncing the carriage along the dirt road. Thanks in large part to the many potholes that slowed the car, Danak and I always won the race.

Automobiles held little interest for me; give me a good horse. By the age of 15, when I would sometimes be entrusted by my father with going out on my own to buy cattle, I took that same two-wheeled carriage, drove it into those little market towns, and went nose to nose with tough old peasants determined to get the best price for their cattle.

I had learned a great deal from Father about negotiating and purchasing strategy. Most important was to have a complete knowledge of the market. What prices were livestock bringing on the wholesale and retail markets?

How much meat did we currently require to fulfill our contract with the army? Would the supply of animals be abundant or scarce in the coming months?

Of course, knowledge alone often did not suffice, especially when competition was especially keen. When Father saw that competitors were in the marketplace, he would often employ some stratagem to get the upper hand. Sometimes he used confederates to visit the farmers, offering them low prices, so that when he came along they thought they were getting a bargain. Or sometimes he would pay an inflated price, more than the competition could afford, even if it meant losing money, simply to drive them out of the market. He would sweep into a market, making 20 or 30 purchases very quickly at a high price. Word would spread among the farmers that Iutcovich was paying such and such, and they would refuse to take the lower price offered by other dealers. But when they came to Father, he would now be offering a lower price, as well. These age-old market place schemes sound as modern as the present-day pricing strategies of giant corporations. They were all new to me and comprised part of my education.

I still recall with considerable pride, after I had an especially successful cattle buying trip on my own, someone commenting to Father, "Your son's a better cattle buyer than you." Father beamed, enormously pleased.

This sort of grassroots capitalism seemed as natural to me as breathing; agriculture seemed to run in my blood. The farm, Danak, the cattle-buying business—for a stretch of years these things were a large part of my life.

Sometimes, when I was on the farm, I would take a lunch to the top of a hill, spread a blanket, and eat there, serene and contemplative. The view encompassed the sprawl of farm buildings and sheep dotting the green pastures. The farm had already fixed itself in my imagination as an oasis of tranquility, a place where I could live and work independently, a place where I could escape. Here, the present seemed uncluttered with school and war; the future seemed as limitless and full of potential as the vista stretching before me.

My mother had already begun talking about medicine as my career. Her sister Elka was practicing medicine in Canada then, and it seemed a noble calling for a gentleman, as well. Medicine had a certain appeal to me, but I was far from firm in my plans. Such weighty decisions seemed too distant to bear.

* * *

"Leon Iutcovich, Director" stood out in bold letters on the frosted glass of the office door. Leon tapped it and smiled, then ushered me from the office to the factory. My brother Leon, having completed his education as a textile engineer, had become a textile manufacturer. With Father's assistance, he purchased this factory in Bucharest.

"We are making cloth that will go into army uniforms," he said, indicating spindles of thread flowing into mechanical looms. A huge open room contained row upon row of women laboring over these machines. Leon provided a running commentary on the material, the machinery, a new contract he had acquired. I was very impressed. With Father as our role model, the entrepreneurial spirit ran deep in our family. Leon would certainly prosper as a manufacturer.

He had also recently married. He and his new wife took an apartment in the city. I was pleased to have family close by and would often visit them. Because of the ten year difference in our ages, Leon and I had seldom spent much time together while growing up. When I was a child, he was a teenager, uninterested in childish things. Then I was off to boarding school and he to the university. When he moved to Bucharest, we were suddenly a fuller, more daily part of each other's life. That made the phone call I received one day from my mother all the more surprising.

"Leon has been beaten up," she told me. "Hurt very badly." The catch in her voice suggested it was serious. He had been taken back home to Braila to convalesce. The moment stabbed deep inside, to a wound ten years old, back to the death of my brother Misa. So young and vital and yet the next moment he was gone, leaving the rest of us to face life without him. Could the same thing happen to Leon?

But one very significant difference separated Misa's circumstances from Leon's. Misa had suffered an accident; Leon had been attacked. Mother only sketched out the details; one did not discuss such things over the phone. But I didn't need to look too far to place blame. Whether he had been beaten by Iron Guard thugs or fascist sympathizers was irrelevant. Whether they attacked Leon because we had Jews in our family or because he employed Jews in his factory, didn't matter either. Such things occurred because of the poisonous presence of the Nazis in Romania. Their twisted Aryan ideology of racial purity incited every manner of crime and cast such a diabolical pall over my country.

I was more incensed than I had ever been in my life. I stayed up late that night drafting a letter to the newspaper, condemning the German presence in Romania and blasting the Nazi ideology as well. I filled it with righteous anger and dramatic statements like ''no foreign boots on our soil,'' and in the morning I slipped it in the mail.

Needless to say, this was not a very prudent thing to do. It represented a dramatic departure from the escapist attitude that I had lived by, in which I tried as much as possible to ignore the ugly atmosphere surrounding me. That event had brought me to a bursting point and robbed me of every ounce of prudence.

The letter appeared in the newspaper a few days later and created a minor stir. Father found out about it and was angry. He could not vent the entire force of his displeasure over the phone, but the next time he came to Bucharest he gave me a stern lecture. ''You feel better now. You wrote your letter. But you didn't think before you acted. You could be their next victim.'' Nor, he explained, had I thought what problems this might cause for the family. That was such a consuming fear for him during the war, and judging from what had befallen Leon, a justified fear.

I worried about consequences for a few days, whether official reaction or the vigilante justice exacted by the Iron

Guard might come down upon me. It never did. The incident gave me pause to consider how my personality was different than my father's. He could certainly be stirred to anger, but he was far more careful in how he expressed it. Whereas my temper flared and drove me towards impulsive actions, without regard for the consequences, Father's anger rarely overrode his reason. He weighed the consequences and the long-term effects before acting. I never quite learned that lesson from Father.

Of course, life is a series of lessons. We are all perpetual students of what life has to teach us. But our basic personalities dictate how effectively we absorb and apply those lessons. I learned much from my father, but have not always applied those lessons as carefully as required. At this point in my life, our circumstances were about to change so dramatically that not even Father could anticipate the necessary lessons.

If I didn't suffer any repercussions on this occasion, maybe it was because the Nazis were too filled with other concerns to worry about one angry letter from a Romanian school boy. Allied bombers were striking deep into the heart of Germany. The long- anticipated Allied invasion of Europe had gotten a toehold in France. Plus, Germany's "glorious" invasion of the Soviet Union had run the course from swift victory to delay, disappointment, and now disaster.

The day the war came to Bucharest, I was in my dorm room studying. The drone of heavy planes broke into my concentration. An excited buzz passed among my school mates as some of them hurried outside. I joined them. We scanned horizon to horizon, but saw nothing. Just the threatening hum of engines filled the air, like a storm of giant insects approaching beyond the horizon.

Then someone pointed up at . . . what was it? Snow or confetti? We couldn't tell. But, like a magical apparition, it mesmerized us as it glinted in the sun, fluttering from the sky. Shortly, came the rumble of bombs striking somewhere in the distance. The war had entered a new phase for us.

After the fact, we learned that there had been a bombing raid on the oil center at Ploesti, approximately 40 kilometers away, and that the bombers had struck as well at the rail yards in Bucharest, dropping bits of tin foil to confuse Romanian radar.

For Romania, the end of the war came quickly. In the East, the Red Army made dramatic gains. A friend who had served in the Romanian Army, would later tell me of the difficulty of resisting the Soviet advance. He said that our army killed wave after wave of charging Red soldiers. "We mowed them down with machine guns. They kept coming, and we kept killing." Finally, said my friend, our army got tired and retreated, assuming that the Russians had more soldiers than we had bullets.

Then, one day, the Germans were gone. It seemed to happen overnight. No more Nazi soldiers on the streets, no more swastika flags fluttering from their cars. Instantly, all outward evidence of their presence disappeared. Romania made a swift change of allegiance and joined the Allied cause just in time to welcome the victorious Red Army.

My friend's description of the Red Army as endless waves of soldiers seemed especially appropriate to their arrival on the scene. When they poured into Romania, they came as a continuous surge, traveling on every possible conveyance. Suddenly, they were everywhere, walking, riding horses, rumbling along in carts, cars, tanks, and old, battered trucks, as if impelled by some great momentum that would not be denied by lack of transportation. Romanians had no great love for their traditional enemy Russia, and many people were fearful of what the Red Army's occupation would portend.

Romanian leader Ion Antonescu was removed in a coup d'etat on August 23, 1944. That same month there came a knock at our door in Braila. Standing there when we opened up was a young officer, dressed in the tunic top and jodhpur trousers of the Red Army. He was dirty and disheveled. We had been expecting him, having earlier been notified that we would be required to quarter a Soviet officer. Both of my parents, having lived in Russian-controlled Bessarabia, spoke fluent Russian. From listening to them speak it at home, I too knew the language.

The Russian officer greeted us in Russian, and we invited him in. We had little idea at that time that we were opening the door to our future.

4
The New World Begins

The Russian soldier threw down another swallow of vodka, mumbled a drunken remark, then fired his machine gun at the ceiling of the hotel dining room. The hotel guests froze in terror as plaster dust drifted in the air. They had seen enough Russian soldiers to be wary of them, but now they were face to face with a madman, a drunken madman, from the army occupying their country. He could act as ruthlessly as he liked—he could even shoot them—and there was nothing they could do.

Unfortunately, this soldier was my traveling companion, assigned as a guard for my father and me as we traveled the countryside buying cattle. Whether his crazed look and brutish behavior were long-standing traits or a product of the war, we didn't know. I tended to believe the latter. This was not the first time we had watched him shoot up a hotel. On this occasion, the Soviet officer, also traveling with us, calmed him down, took away his gun, and the man went back to drowning his rage in vodka. I remember thinking, "What a strange world we have entered."

Crushing reparations were being exacted from Romania to cover Soviet losses during the war and to maintain the occupying forces. Cattle made up part of the reparation payments. Father had won a huge contract with the Romanian government to oversee a large part of the reparations effort. He was charged with buying cattle for delivery to the Red Army. Also, he operated warehouses to store meat for distribution to the occupying Red Army.

We must have made an interesting sight, crowded into Father's well-appointed Chevrolet, with the chauffeur and two Russian soldiers, as we drove our old routes, and visited the same market towns. The Soviet officer was a decent fellow, a Jew from Leningrad. His father was a cantor. We became fast friends, drinking and carousing during these trips. These guards were to protect us from other Soviet troops. Their presence signaled that we were on official business, and saved us from being harassed or robbed by the other soldiers we encountered on the road.

After a few months, father had gathered a large herd for delivery to the Red Army at the Soviet border. But he had a few tricks in store for the Russians. For several days, he fed the cattle on salt, to raise a powerful thirst. Then he drove them to the river, where they eagerly sucked down gallons of water, making them swell up and add weight. Only then did he deliver them to the border.

We arrived bearing gifts of food and drink for the high-ranking Soviet delegation that awaited us. It had been our experience that Russians did not need an excuse to get drunk; if there was vodka, they would drink, and drink until it was gone. We had brought with us a great deal of vodka.

We shared a meal at a local hotel. Though I was but 16 years old at the time, vodka was pressed upon me, as toast after toast was lifted in forced good will. Cheers to a swift Allied victory! Cheers to Marshall Stalin! Cheers to Soviet-Romanian cooperation! With everyone feeling a besotted brotherhood, we finally got down to the business at hand.

A holding area had been set up with a weighing station. Cattle were led from our herd onto a scale, their weight recorded, and then they joined the Soviet herd. What the Russians didn't realize, amid the confused shuffling of so many cattle, was that Father was circling many of the animals, leading the same ones onto the scale two or three times.

It was so unlike Father to be dishonest. I said to him, "That's cheating."

He shook his head. "No. That's patriotism. Why should we give away our wealth?"

When I wasn't traveling with Father, I worked in one of our warehouses. Since I spoke Russian, I dealt with the Soviet procurement officer when he came to take deliveries of meat. Here we also had a scheme to cheat the Red Army, but we worked it with the cooperation of the Soviet officer. I would weigh up some meat for delivery to the Red Army, say 200 kilograms. But I would write 400 kilograms on the invoice. The officer would sign it and receive a bribe for his cooperation.

* * *

It was still possible to believe, as we worked our familiar routine in those early months after the war ended for Romania, that everything would be all right. World War II would come to an end, we would pay off the Russians and they would depart, then, free of fascists and Communists, Romania would rise phoenix-like from the rubble.

For any clear-thinking individual—I was not always clear-thinking—this dream became increasingly hard to believe. In March of 1945, a Communist-dominated coalition government took power. Membership in the Romanian Communist Party soared, less from genuine sympathizers than from realists who had no delusions about how long the Soviets would stay.

"The best Nazis make the best Communists," my father would often grumble, in reference to the political opportunists who were so quick to embrace the ideology *du jour*. Russia had long been a traditional enemy of Romania; it was easy to hate the presence of its occupying army and the Communist ideology they brought with them. But life had to go on; people had to adapt to the circumstances. And circumstances tokened a Communist future for Romania.

Father saw the writing on the wall long before I did. We had a such a good life, and I did not want to admit that we could lose it. Early on he spoke of selling off assets and moving money out of the country. But I convinced him not to, even persuaded him to put more money into the farm. Never before in my young life had I held so fast to a belief. After all, King Michael was still on the throne. Europe had only begun the process of picking up the pieces from the war. The Allies would stop any attempt by the Soviet Union to seize control in Romania, I reasoned. Everything would sort itself out, and our lives would return to the way they had been.

So, I went on with my life, with my plans to enter the university. Education in Romania was free and based upon merit. Periodically, throughout your schooling, you were given comprehensive tests. Fail them and you could not continue, pass them and you went on to the next level. These occurred at the end of elementary school, before entering high school, and to gain entrance to the university.

The tests were formal and frightening affairs, administered at an official testing site. On your desk sat your photograph, to assure your identity, and a sealed envelope holding the test. Because so much depended on them, anxiety was high. It was not unusual for students to be so nervous that they vomited or wet their pants.

After completing high school, students took their baccalaureate exams. I traveled to the town of Galatz for testing, first a grueling written exam, then an oral examination. Ten of us sat in a row, terrified, while several professors shot questions at us. We recited Latin verses, answered questions on literature and history, and experiments in physics.

Mother had convinced me to pursue a career in medicine, and so, after completing my baccalaureate, I took an entrance exam for the university medical school. That year 10,000 students vied for 100 seats in medical school. I was fortunate to be one of those granted admission.

Unfortunately, my interests and temperament did not lie in medicine. Once during the classroom dissection of a cadaver, I passed out. This was a common occurrence, I was assured. But when it happened again while I was observing an operation, I took this as a sign that the life of a physician was not for me. I changed my course of study to sociology. I did not tell my mother of this until much later.

Mother's opinion, and her anger, were still powerful forces influencing my behavior.

Only one souvenir survived from my medical student days. Somewhere along the way I had picked up a cyanide capsule, a tiny glass pill that could kill in an instant, the sort that spies bit into at dramatic moments in B-movies. I don't know why I held onto it, but I tucked it away in my desk drawer. Years later it would become my most valued possession.

From the very start, sociology captured my interest. I wanted to learn how people interacted, how they were influenced and controlled. The examples of fascism and Communism had given ample demonstration of how effectively this could be done. After taking my first test in this new curriculum, I received a summons from the professor, a man named Stahl, to visit him at home. He was a very well-known scholar because of his studies in rural sociology. He had created a peasant museum, really a peasant village, set aside to study this way of life.

I was very nervous, fearful that he had bad news for me, perhaps that I had done poorly on the test and must leave the program. Of course, given the exalted status that professors enjoyed, I was also nervous just to be sitting down with him. We met in the garden of his home, over a cup of tea. He praised my performance on the test and asked if I would be his assistant. I was enormously flattered that he would even consider me for the position. I accepted his offer, and thus began a rewarding relationship, through which I received much encouragement.

Sociology would stimulate in me a social activism and an interest in politics. Of course, it was hard to escape politics in those post-war years. Winston Churchill had already popularized the term "iron curtain" for the boundary between East and West that now extended across Europe. In the west, the United States was rebuilding Europe with the Marshall Plan. In Eastern Europe, the Soviet Union was recreating countries in its own image. Cold War tensions were replacing the tensions of World War II.

In Romania, the forced collectivization of agriculture had gotten underway. The Communists were flexing their muscles, forcing a free people and a free country to fit their ideological mold. They had no compunction about taking the lives of all who resisted them. From 1946 through 1947, an estimated 40,000-60,000 Romanians died at the hands of their own government.

During my first year at the University, my brother Leon was my closest confidante. We worried over these things together. However, these seismic political changes had not yet shaken the foundations of education. My professors were still free to teach what they wished and to express their opinions, though perhaps with a bit more circumspection than before. And the new government still needed capitalists like Leon and my father to make the economy function.

Instead, our worries took a different turn early in 1947, when Leon fell ill with a nasty cold. He took to bed and plied himself with the usual medications. But it hung on, and got worse, and was finally determined to be leukemia. That diagnosis galvanized the family. Leukemia was almost always fatal. My parents immediately came to Bucharest to be with him. Having already lost one son while they were absent, they were not about to have it happen again. They would take charge of his care, be meticulous in their attention to his cure, do everything humanly possible to see him through this affliction.

The family kept a vigil at Leon's hospital bed. I remember it as a strange capsule of time, or rather of time standing still. Everything was put on hold. Nothing existed outside that hospital. All of our attention, every ounce of our strength was devoted to the one, overriding goal of restoring Leon to health. Despite our efforts, his condition worsened.

Father got the names of eminent medical experts in France and Canada and consulted with them. They were not encouraging, but they steered him towards the latest wonder drug—penicillin. It had been used effectively during the War to fight infections, and the full effects of its powers had not yet been determined. Perhaps—just perhaps—it could prevent the inevitable outcome usually associated with leukemia. However, penicillin was very scarce. None existed in Romania. Father had to charter an airplane to fly penicillin from France to Bucharest, where it was immediately administered to my brother.

I can't remember whether the penicillin had any effect at all; I only recall the outcome—Leon died.

I want to put my finger on that very moment when my brother breathed his last and vest it with great importance. I want to say, "*Here* is the great divide in my life. Before that moment, optimism and purpose filled me. After that moment, the world turned upside down, and something in me did as well. But if losing a second brother upset my emotional life, it was Communism's strengthening grip on my country that upset day-to-day existence.

My parents had buried my brother Misa but they cremated Leon, a nod to the uncertainty of life in those postwar years. It would not do to put another son in the ground in Braila if we would eventually leave the country. But any thoughts of leaving the country took a back seat to mourning. For all practical purposes, my parents locked themselves away for a year. They both stayed home; Father conducted little business.

From then on, things were not the same in our home. There was no more laughter. All the juice, the flare for life that had so animated both of my parents, had disappeared. Almost as a way to compensate for their withdrawal from life, I threw myself into it. I too felt the tragedy of Leon's loss, but I did not want to accept it as closing the door on the rest of life. So, I preferred to busy myself with work and friends.

As usual in summer, Bebu came back into my life. Bebu was an amazingly unflappable person. The comparison to a monk comes to mind. Through war and repression, while the rest of us were buffeted by problems large and small, Bebu stands out as the benchmark of calm, intellectual detachment.

He was a good listener and would sometimes share personal things, but then we would shake that off and he would press upon me some book, as though literature was the only constant in life, the rudder to steer one through life's storms. In that summer of 1947, Bebu had me and some of my friends reading Tolstoy's *Anna Karenina*.

But my interests became directed elsewhere that summer. Staying at the farm so often, tending to some of the duties Father was neglecting, I had much contact with Stefan, the Greek who managed things there, and his wife, Katty. One evening when I was eating supper with them, Katty began stroking my leg with her foot. That was an awkward moment, with Stefan right there, talking about the farm, while Katty set my hormones to boil. I reciprocated, and it would be the overture that launched an affair between us.

Both of us seemed primed for this to happen. I had no serious girlfriend at the time. There had been little pleasure in my life since Leon's death. The uncertainty of the postwar world seemed to rob meaning from life, making me more likely to grab at immediate pleasures. It was escapism, the principle form of pleasure in an unsettled life.

I didn't know Katty's motives, but they propelled her just as strongly into this passionate relationship. We grabbed pleasure whenever and wherever we could—in the house, the barn, the fields—as though stealing happiness quickly and secretively from a world that would otherwise begrudge it to us.

Back in Braila, when we discussed *Anna Karenina*, someone would ask me, "What do you think of Anna's affair with Count Vronsky?" and I would offer something about how Tolstoy made it seem acceptable, even inevitable. "You are made to care more for the lover than for the husband," I pointed out.

As in much of Tolstoy's work, social commentary wove through the plot of this novel. Your sympathies are drawn to Anna, and yet she is an adulteress. She is willing to court scandal, jeopardize her marriage and her husband's social standing for love. Should Anna be condemned for so selfish an attitude that holds the individual above society or was her society at fault for forcing her into such an untenable position?

These were the very issues Tolstoy meant to raise, and they framed the nature of our discussion of the book. The passing resemblance to my own relationship with Katty was not lost on me. My own affair did not seem raised to so exalted a plane as Anna's, and yet it flaunted some of the same conventions with an adulterous relationship.

It was Bebu's idea for us to stage a courtroom drama based upon the book—to put Anna Karenina on trial. This was not to be a simple literary exercise among friends, but a public performance staged in an auditorium. Such literary entertainments were common. Bebu's suggestion won instant approval. Anna's predicament has appeal in any age or place, but especially so under repressive governments, where an individual's rights can stand in sharp conflict with social obligations. I volunteered to be Anna's defense attorney.

I remember the tragic story of poor Anna Karenina so well. A woman trapped in a loveless marriage, in love with another man. Because of his own social and political standing, the husband will not consider the scandal of a divorce. Anna chooses to be with her lover, is scorned by society, loses custody of her son, and eventually commits suicide publicly, a gesture meant to punish her oppressors.

Through Anna and other characters in the novel, Tolstoy seems to suggest that following one's passion leads to tragedy. However, in my arguments, I placed the blame on society. Anna was simply a victim of laws and social conventions that favored men, that allowed her no route to happiness, that doomed her new relationship, and led to her suicide.

I really can't recall if I won the decision for poor Anna that night. But I firmly believed my arguments. One didn't have to extrapolate too far beyond Anna's circumstances to see the broader issue of the individual standing against society. Perhaps it was only my fertile, adolescent imagination, but tension seemed to simmer in the auditorium that night, as though in Anna's moral dilemma the audience saw a reflection of some painful decision that might face each of them as Romania's repressive Communist government established itself.

I do recall that my parents attended the performance. They had become increasingly attentive to and indulgent of me since losing Leon. With grief and the changing economic climate still preventing Father from actively pursuing his business, their whole world had dramatically narrowed. I was happy to see them in the audience that night, happy for their support.

Meanwhile, constant energy drove my interests in ever broader and wilder pursuits. Though I was "involved" with Katty, we were not in love in the traditional sense; we did not speak of a life together. I was a young man now and had money at my disposal. I dated many women, attended parties, and threw parties.

Among the mother of eligible young women in Braila, I acquired a poor reputation. Perhaps they had heard some of the wild stories about Mark Iutcovich. Perhaps things were whispered about my affair with Katty. Perhaps they had heard about the time that I and a date got wildly drunk, disrobed, mounted two horses and rode through a local village, hooting and hollering, making the peasants think that the devil himself had paid a visit.

One of my exploits became legend in the region, the time I rented an entire hotel and restaurant at a Black Sea resort for a wild week of revelry. I sold off livestock from the family farm to finance the event. Dozens of friends and acquaintances turned out, and we partied as though there would never again be a celebration like this, as though tomorrow would never arrive.

The local newspaper carried a story about the wild party back to the good people of Braila, who gossiped about it for a long time afterward. Father took the party in stride but he was angered by the fact that I had taken with me the daughter of one of his friends. I had embarrassed him with his friends, something you did not do.

Not surprisingly, among the good families of Braila, I had a reputation for not being a very serious young man, certainly not a serious candidate for a son-in-law.

In hindsight, there was more at issue than just wild antics. My seaside escapade reminds me a bit of Boccaccio's *The Decameron*, whose premise was that a group of young people escape to a villa outside Florence to avoid a plague raging in the city. There they take turns being monarch for a day and tell stories, some quite lascivious.

It was not plague that the youth of Romania sought to escape in 1947 but a strange political twilight that existed, an *inter regnum* between two forms of government that seemed to heighten their predisposition to teenage wildness. The traditional patterns governing life in the Old Romania, with its constitutional monarchy, were being replaced by Communism. The old values of the village, the work ethic, the concept of private property, the very notion of planning for the future—all of these were being redefined or abandoned. We knew only that a shadow was descending over our lives and that tomorrow would be different in a way that we did not yet fully understand.

In the face of this turmoil, Father's mind was thinking of how to salvage his wealth and make his escape from Romania. My thoughts ran only to escapism. The inevitable changes about to alter my way of life forever were too confusing and painful to confront, and so I sought out distractions. If there was some way to wring out the last few drops of pleasure from this lifestyle before it disappeared forever, then I found it. That's what kept me going in the face of the ugly events occurring in that year.

A maniacal bastard named Nicolae Ceausescu was leading the ruthless collectivization of agriculture with a simple policy: confiscate all private farms, and kill all those who resisted. My father had begun to quietly liquidate assets and transfer funds out of the country.

Some of my acquaintances had even begun to change their perceptions of Communism. Perhaps it was not so bad, they began to say; and anyway, it was our future. Hearing such things angered me. Sometimes I flew back at them and called them blind or ignorant. Other times their arguments for accepting the inevitable rang with impotent logic, and I just quietly cursed their weakness.

I have always resented the ideological "flexibility" of my countryman. You can not fault those who embraced Communism because they truly believed that it would deliver on its humanitarian promises. But, those tempted by the advantages of Party membership who were willing to ignore the abuses and crimes of the government simply to better their own position—what can you say about them?

Everyone faced that sort of decision in those years. What do I think of Communism? What should I do? What will my position be? Over dinner at his house, my friend Emil confessed a sympathy for the ideals of Communism—universal brotherhood, sharing the wealth of society. Ideals are one thing, I said, but the reality is altogether different.

"I have joined the Party," he announced to me sometime later, taking a defensive tone that anticipated my criticism. When I didn't attack, he revealed his reasoning. He would work within the Party to do good. He would steer Communism on the right course in Romania. His face shone with conviction. I could see that he truly believed what he was saying. "Join with me, Mark," he begged. "Help me to do this." What do you say to such a person, when they are beyond logic? It was a painful evening.

I declined his offer and went home that night in a great depression. It felt all the world as though I had just lost my friend, as totally and irrevocably as I had lost Leon. What were these other people seeing in Communism that I did not? Their practical arguments about Communism being inevitable in Romania might well be true, but that was certainly no reason to embrace a repressive, terroristic regime. If that were so, we would have linked arms with the Nazis.

Unless, of course, you could rationalize your way around such terrorism as the unfortunate means necessary to achieve the final goal of a classless utopia. For me that was ludicrous. Try as I might, I could not understand their thinking.

But such thinking was a contagion that slowly gripped more of those I knew and cared for. One by one over the next year, my friends Emil, Ion, and Silviu joined the ranks of the Party, making me feel progressively more isolated. Some of those friendships continued, but they were different after that.

What an appropriate refrain for 1947—forever, life would be different after that year.

5
The Communist Takeover

That fall when I returned to school, I launched a campaign to be elected student government president. In Romania this was a national office, presidency of all the students attending Romania's four universities, in Bucharest, Cluj, Timisoara, Jassy. Although Romania was a bubbling cauldron of politics that fall, this campaign dealt with the typical concerns of students: better conditions in the dormitories, better food in the cafeterias. One did not speak publicly about politics.

I discovered that I had a skill for public speaking and for organizing the details of a campaign, at least enough skill to win that election. The pieces of my life seemed to come together in that victory, as though it opened a glimpse of my future. I thrilled to the prospect of rolling up my sleeves and tackling the problems of concern to students, and rubbing elbows with national politicians. I imagined that the negotiating skills learned in the cattle markets would serve me well in this post.

My duties took me to the Education Ministry offices in Bucharest. I would go there to represent the needs of the students, or sometimes summoned by politicians hoping that I could deliver student votes for an election.

This plunge into national politics made me consider pursuing a political career. Maybe this was where I had been heading all along, I thought. Maybe my early education and experiences, my current studies of sociology, and my father's considerable reputation were the steps to high office. In idle moments that fall, I fantasized about becoming president of Romania and guiding it through those troubled times. Of course, many a young man dreams of becoming president of his country, but for a brief period that fall I truly thought that it was possible and within my reach.

I could not have picked a more ill-conceived moment in Romanian history to indulge such a dream. Barbarians were at the gate.

The Communists made their power grab for the government that fall in their typically brutish way, by eliminating all opposition. Mass jailings and liquidations had been going on for some time. In August, the National Peasant and National Liberal parties had been dissolved and their leaders convicted of "anti-state" activities. Currency reforms undertaken that same month, devastated the value of bank deposits. Father was thankful that he had been able to get a significant sum of money into a Swiss bank.

This political turmoil spilled over to the university. Throughout the fall, debates became increasingly heated and angry. In dormitories, hallways, cafeterias, wherever students gathered, you were likely to find the factions arguing, or more likely yelling, at each other. Arguments against Communism came primarily from two camps: the Nationalists, supporters of the old fascist government; and those favoring democracy. Clinging to the waning prestige of my student presidency, I argued strongly for the practice of democracy in the university and the government.

But matters had already gone beyond debate. No one seriously discussed issues any more. Instead, confrontations degenerated into angry, threatening exchanges. The Party had already gained a strong presence in the university with its youth group, the Young Communists. More and more power seemed to be gravitating towards them. I became something of a champion for the voice of opposition, a role that I did not seek nor deserve. After one especially hostile encounter my supporters provided me with body guards to protect against possible retaliation from Party supporters.

But the writing was on the wall. Our squabbling counted for nothing in the unfolding drama. In December,

King Michael was forced to abdicate. The Romanian Peoples Republic came into existence in January 1948.

Just as Communism transformed the country, so it transformed the university. Students who joined the Young Communists were given membership cards and accorded certain privileges. Most students joined, and it angered me to see them flock like sheep to a cause that a short time before they had found unpalatable. Political commissars appeared on the scene, and informers monitored students for any improper conduct or attitude. Every subject of study now had to have an ideological connection. Textbooks had to be rewritten, lecture notes recomposed, to provide a Marxist interpretation to the curriculum. Those professors who resisted were removed. You came to class one day, in the middle of term, and a new professor might be there to greet you. No explanation given, none needed. The important lesson about Communism—that it tolerated no opposition—had already been amply demonstrated in a thousand ways.

Today, when I read in the paper about a school district or an outside group that wants to impose an ideology onto the curriculum—"creationism," for instance—it rouses clear and painful memories of 1948.

* * *

"Join the Party," my friends urged me anew. Silviu joined, then Ion. We met at restaurants, and they tried to talk some sense into me. "The time has come. This was Romania's future." But I could not be persuaded. This was just another form of my escapism, clinging to the hope that Communism would not triumph and I would not have to make such hard decisions.

Ion was now dating my old girlfriend, Phylicia. The three of us met in a restaurant. Phylicia's jailbird boyfriend had fled the country, and she had taken up with Ion, a good Party member who would have a future and could protect her. "There are career opportunities in the Party," Ion said. I had only the warmest regards for my old friend

Ion and had no more attachment to Phylicia, so I wished them well, but said that I was unable to bring myself to join the Party.

Outside the university, armed resistance groups had formed, headquartered in the Carpathian Mountains. These "partisans" hoped to overthrow the new government by military struggle. This became the popular cause for some of the students I knew. I still recall one of them, Georgi, a Greek-Romanian, so filled with the romantic notion of guerilla war, so convinced that a just cause would win out over tyranny. He planned to drop out of the university and join the fight and begged me to go with him.

"You're crazy," I told him. "I don't want to be a dead hero. The Russians have tens of thousands of troops all over the country. You can't fight them." He went to fight anyway. I said good bye, wished him well, and never saw him again. Regularly in the newspaper, articles appeared about skirmishes between the army and the "Nazi Reactionaries," as the government called the partisans. Three partisans dead, five or ten partisans killed—the result was always the same. Whenever I read such accounts, I wondered if one of those bodies was Georgi.

For those of us who clung to the hope that the West would step in to resist this Communist takeover, the foreign radio broadcasts we listened to offered no hope. The spring of 1948 saw a Communist-led civil war in China, and Communist coups d'etat in Hungary and Czechoslovakia. My old friends had been right on one score; it appeared that Communism would be Romania's fate.

* * *

Father had resolved that Canada would be our new home. For years, we had been in touch with Mother's sister Elka, who had settled in Winnipeg and established a flourishing medical practice. Given the dramatic turn of events in Romania since the War, the freedom of the West had an enormous appeal. Father was intrigued by the business opportunities.

We knew that there would be no problem acquiring visas to enter Canada, the only problem would be getting a passport to leave Romania. No clear policy seemed to have emerged yet on who would be permitted to leave and under what circumstances, so we applied and waited.

My parents lived in a state of perpetual anxiety that summer as we waited to hear word on our request for passports. Father labored desperately to liquidate his remaining assets. Somewhere, in some office, some Party functionaries sat over a map, plotting which properties the government would seize next. The government officer in charge of nationalizing property around Braila was of gypsy origin. He visited our farm on several occasions and assured me that it was only a matter of time. "Do not be here when they come," he warned, "because they will arrest you."

I stayed at the farm a good deal that summer. I believed the official, but put off facing the inevitable. Plus, we were desperate to liquidate as much of our livestock as possible. Whatever we did not dispose of or carry away from the farm, would fall into government hands. If I had any doubts about that, the gypsy official would put them to rest on one of his visits. "I'm warning you, Iutcovich. The time is near. Unless you like prison, don't be here."

Of course, there were no buyers for the house or farm—the government would soon own them. But, we continued to butcher animals and sell the meat. A collective farm bought some of our horses. My old leanings towards escapism reasserted themselves. I ignored the gathering clouds of doom, dividing my attentions between the farm and my continuing involvement with Katty.

One night after I had just gone to bed, one of the workers came pounding at the door. "They are coming to take the farm!" he yelled. "They are just down the road!" I jumped to action, cursing myself for having delayed my departure. Not even pausing to don clothing, I ran to the barn in my pajamas, jumped bareback onto a horse and galloped away.

I didn't know if they would pursue me, so I kept up a fast pace all the way back to Braila, where I informed my parents. It was the final straw for my father. The final collapse that he had worried about since the end of the war, had finally occurred. Our life in Braila, all that he had built up there, was now over.

The appropriateness of our decision to leave Romania could not have been better confirmed. I moved to my apartment in Bucharest. Some evenings I would sit on the apartment balcony, looking out at the city, fretting about the future. Those occasions would bring to mind my first night alone in Bucharest, when Father had first taken me to boarding school, how I had peered out the window of the dormitory at the expanse of the city. Back then, Bucharest had appeared so huge and intimidating and at the same time so exciting, filled with delicious mystery and opportunity.

Now, it stirred more ominous feelings in me. I might as well have been on the moon as on a balcony for how distant I felt from the city and the life it represented. Emotionally, I had already abandoned my life in Romania. I only waited for my ticket out.

Shortly thereafter, my parents also moved to Bucharest. Another couple from Braila was also awaiting passports to leave the country. They had a small apartment in the city. My parents moved in with them, while we waited. And waited. Months went by. Anxiety rose. What if we would not be allowed to leave the country? What then?

Meanwhile, the house in Braila was nationalized, as was my apartment in Bucharest. I was permitted to remain in my apartment, but a young couple and a single man moved in with me. We each had a room, but shared a kitchen and bath. How many family arguments and bouts of love making did I share with them through those thin walls. How many times did I interrupt the same when I was forced to cross one of their rooms to use the toilet. Communism certainly put us on more intimate terms with our neighbors.

Life continued its transformation. Shortages appeared everywhere. One needed ration coupons to buy food. Coupons were issued through your place of employment or your school. If you were not employed or not attending school, you did not get coupons. At the university, only Party members received coupons. Restaurants, too, had been nationalized, but you could still buy a meal there without a coupon.

A version of the "fast food" restaurant appeared for the first time. Called "canteens," they catered to workers on a short meal break who had to grab a quick bite to eat. We ate there frequently. Food was also available on the black market. The black market had existed during the war but it was now establishing itself as a permanent part of life. Harsh penalties existed to punish the black market "economic saboteurs." But, unlike Romania's new *regulated* economy, the black market *free* economy actually worked. Like so much else at that time, layers were forming: an official economy and a hidden economy, an official version of reality, and the truth.

Word finally came from the government—my parents had gotten their passports, but my request had been denied. No explanation. Perhaps they thought my father was an irreclaimable capitalist, while I, being young, could still be molded into an acceptable Communist. My father made persistent inquiries but got nowhere. My mother refused to leave without me. It was not worth leaving if she lost her only remaining child in the bargain.

The only reason I was not as distraught as Mother was because I had already begun fabricating escape plans. Within a few days of having my passport request denied, I began my exercise swims. I swam laps at one of the city swimming pools, working to increase my endurance, and practicing especially to the lengthen the distance I could swim underwater. This is how I would take leave of my country.

At Braila, I swam the Danube to further challenge my endurance. The river was about half a kilometer wide. Back and forth across that great river, I would often cover 15 kilometers in one swimming session.

When I stood on the banks of the river, breathless after a gruelling swim, I would imagine that I had travelled to the southeast corner of Romania, where for a hundred kilometers or so, the Danube serves as the border with Yugoslavia. In my mind, I stood on the river bank, filling my lungs before plunging in and swimming across.

All the while Father and I were convincing Mother she must leave, that I would follow shortly. Even though she finally relented, we nearly had to drag her to the airport on the day of departure. We shed a lot of tears while waiting for their plane. They were heading off for a new life and all its uncertainty; I was staying behind in a new Romania, with even more uncertainty. And, worst of all, we were separating.

At the airport, her face glistening with tears, Mother held my head, looked me square in the eyes, and said, "Don't do anything foolish." It was a reference, I knew, to my idea of swimming my way out of Romania, or to even more fanciful, and dangerous escape plans that might take form in my imagination. She tried to imbue her admonition with her old brand of authority, but it came off as more of a desperate plea. She had already lost two sons, and couldn't bare the thought of losing me as well.

My parents flew off to Paris, where my father's sister lived. I possess one photograph from their months of Parisian exile. It is of them walking in the warm light of a park. If their expression is not exactly one of happiness, at least they look more at ease than they had looked for a long time during their final days in Romania. They would remain in Paris for nearly six months before finally moving to Winnipeg, Canada to start over as immigrants in a new land. The more than $400,000 that my father had managed to pile up in a Swiss bank account would assure them a comfortable life.

Not long after my parents left I saw a newspaper article about Yugoslavia returning some Romanians who had tried to escape their country. All my plans of escape took on the substance of daydreams after that.

But I had one final, far more realistic, plan for leaving Romania. I had a very close friend in high government office. Someone from whom I could seek assistance in acquiring a passport. My long-time friend Emil had early on embraced the Party and had risen quickly to an important position in the Interior Ministry, working for state security. He had become something of a protege to Teohari Georgescu, a member of the Party's inner circle. I knew that he had the power to give me a passport, if he chose to. I went to visit him at his lavish office in downtown Bucharest.

I spoke to him as a friend, explaining the circumstances, the confiscation of property, my parents leaving the country, my denied passport, my own untenable position in Romania since I was not a Party member, and I asked for his help in getting a passport. I sensed, as I made my plea, that it was not reaching that long-ago bond of friendship, that an insurmountable obstacle now stood between us.

When I concluded, Emil's face contorted with anger. "If I didn't remember that you were my friend," he growled, "I would throw you in prison, and you would never see the sun again."

Perhaps it was a mark of my own naiveté that his response so surprised and angered me. Throughout the past year as one after the other of my friends joined the Party, I had been disappointed but not angry. I remember one of them, a Jew, telling me that the Party dealt fairly with everyone, regardless of religion, and that for the first time he would be on equal footing with others. They all had practical reasons for joining, and I certainly did not hold it against them. They were still my friends; they were still human beings.

But Emil had been transformed. Some elemental spark of humanity had been drained from him in the process of indoctrination. It caused me to explode. I had never before in my life felt such hateful rage for anyone. At that moment, he represented for me everything that was repugnant about

Communism. I must have yelled at and cursed him for half an hour. I felt better when it was over, but it didn't change the outcome. I left without a passport and with one less friend.

*   *   *

Finishing out the rest of my education became a great chore. The term "intellectual prostitution" was never more aptly applied than to the transformation of education under Communism. Truth, accuracy, fairness, competence, and the pursuit of knowledge took a back seat to following the Party line. Just as purges continued throughout the rest of society, uncooperative professors disappeared from the classroom. Those that remained were either ardent followers of the faith, or they were scared enough to fill their lectures and their scholarly work with political claptrap.

Members of the Young Communists could get by without attending class, if they claimed to be on Party business. No professor would be brazen enough to fail any of them. I played the game. I wrote out the standard Marxist responses in papers and test questions and managed to muddle through. But the thrill of intellectual achievement that had been so dear to me was no longer there. The process had become a sham. My interest fell off, and my attendance declined, as I marked time until graduation.

The only income I had during this time came from my parents. It arrived through the British embassy. Every month, a letter came in the post from the embassy, all done very discretely. No Romanian could have contact with a foreign embassy. So the letter arrived in a nondescript envelope, a check for 1,000 leis, about $100, drawn on a Romanian bank.

But 1000 leis did not go very far. My biggest expense was food. Since I was not a Party member, I did not receive food coupons to allow for purchase of food in government stores. I either ate in restaurants or bought on the black market, at higher prices. Some things, such as bread, were available without coupons, as was produce in season. Still, my resources were stretched very thin. I had to find a way to get additional income.

One of the very few sources of freelance work available at the time was in translating. A Soviet bookstore had opened in Bucharest. There was a rush to translate many Soviet volumes into Romanian. I set about polishing up my Russian, and within seven or eight months, had mastered it well enough to translate technical books.

I would take my meager earning from translating and trek off to one of those apartments in the city where I knew a black marketer would have produce or meat for sale. Strange how the profit motive made food appear in this clandestine economy, even when the shelves in the government stores were empty.

I could also make purchases at one of the unofficial marketplaces that were tolerated in Bucharest, where peasants sold produce. Peasants were not permitted to own farms, but they could have small plots of land by their homes to raise produce and keep a few animals.

I became so dependent and familiar with the black market and the fledgling capitalism of these peasant markets that I eventually hatched my own plan of "economic sabotage." I befriended one of the farmers and arranged for the purchase of a pig. This was dangerous business. But desperation is a strong motivator.

I waited late at night outside my apartment building until the farmer arrived in his wagon. He helped me carry the pig to the courtyard behind my building, then left quickly. I killed the pig there, slit its throat above a storm drain, gutted and butchered it, as I had seen done so many times on the farm. If the neighbors wondered about the squealing or the telltale blood visible the next morning, no one ever mentioned it. We had all been well trained not to ask questions. Perhaps it was an enemy of the state being dispatched right there in their own courtyard. In any case, it didn't do to know too much.

I felt a certain satisfaction from learning how to manipulate the system. How to make do on my own terms. How to survive. I had always been one to go my own way. Now

I was demonstrating that I could do it as well under these trying circumstances.

My apartment had a closed in balcony to which only I had a key. I wrapped the meat and stored it there. I had no trouble selling it. But because of the riskiness of such a venture, I only went into the pig business two or three times a year. Despite the extensiveness of the black market, people were arrested all the time for such activities. Those arrested usually became part of the legions who disappeared.

It seems ironic that in a time and place where the term "education" lost most of its meaning, that the Party would popularize the term "re-education." In theory, it was their name for the process of teaching those citizens who resisted the changes of Communism to adopt a new way of thinking, the Party way of thinking. In reality, "re-education" simply meant the elimination of opposition by whatever means necessary, death being the most obvious and frequently employed means.

Most everyone had something to be scared about in those days. I worried about receiving money through the British embassy. I was frightened the night I butchered the pig and during the days that followed when I had kilos of fresh pork in my apartment.

Your imagination takes hold of a paranoia and torments you with worry. You remember the worst stories you have heard of people being killed by the government. In the middle of the night, when sleep won't come, you see the face of a friendly professor who one day failed to return to the classroom. Had he been discharged? Or left the country? Or been imprisoned? You never learned, and the matter planted itself in your brain where you tried to ignore it, tried to fit it into this new reality. You couldn't ask questions about such things. They were not discussed. It struck you at such times, when you butchered pigs in darkened courtyards, and familiar faces disappeared, what a strange world you had fallen into.

Education, farming, the economy, living conditions—nothing remained as it had been. It played havoc with the way you thought of things—traditions were gone, interpersonal relations had been redefined, new social and personal goals were imposed upon the population. Some made a smooth transition; the challenge of adjustment even invigorated some. Personally, I felt victimized, not only for the loss of property and a comfortable way of life, but for the loss of our national culture. Not only for the loss of the past—that was bad enough—but for the loss of the future.

And the present? It was recast in the false reality of the "Party line." Truth was falsehood. Reality was fantasy. Bad was good. It all depended on how you looked at it, how the Party interpreted it. The "True Believers" had taken over. They knew the truth, the things it was proper to believe, the way to live life and organize society. To disagree meant that you were the enemy, of the government and the people. True believers have existed throughout history; they certainly exist today. The tragedy occurs when they are in a position to force their beliefs on others.

This mysterious shrinking of the familiar would continue for the rest of my years in Romania. In time its mysterious quality would cease to catch my attention. Unless it struck close to home—a close acquaintance or colleague disappearing—it became as natural and unremarkable as the weather. People simply disappeared.

Until, that is, it happened to me. Like Alice crawling down the rabbit hole in *Alice in Wonderland* and passing into a strange and unknown world, I too would experience this phenomenon. I would learn where so many of the disappeared had ended up, in a land very strange but more hellish than wonderful. I was about to go there myself. I had no inkling of it, but I too was about to disappear.

6

The Land of the Disappeared

The caller on the telephone said he was from Party headquarters and that the Secretary of the Communist Youth organization wished to see me in his office the next day at 10 a.m. Fleetingly, I thought, "He has rung up the wrong number. I'm not a Party member and have nothing to do with the Communist Youth." But there was no mistake; they wanted to see me.

It was the spring of my senior year at the university, and my future remained an empty horizon. My pending graduation seemed to call for a decision, some action to shape my life. A university degree without Party membership did little to improve one's prospects. The thought of continuing my current circumstances, living on the edge of society, grubbing for poorly-paid translation assignments, slaughtering pigs in the dead of night, depressed me.

I had heard of people who hired guides to lead them along risky escape routes across the border, through Yugoslavia and to freedom in Austria, and I thought longingly of making that trip. I had recently resumed my swimming regimen, as if that old fantasy of escape, improbable as it was, provided some small light of hope to illuminate those dark days. But, too often I had seen newspaper accounts of failed escape attempts that had landed people in prison. Regardless of how difficult circumstances were for me, they were much preferable to prison.

So, in that spring of 1950 I was waiting for my future to unfold. I had no plans and no prospects, just a summons to appear at Party headquarters.

"Wait here," the guard said, installing me in a chair facing a desk in a large office. The minutes crept by, and no one appeared. My throat was dry, my heart drumming at a lively rate. My spinning imagination would not settle on just one worry. I knew how Communists thought, and knew there was much in my background to disturb them. My father had been a capitalist landowner with all the trappings of bourgeois success. I recalled some of the debates at the university where I had too boldly criticized the changes brought about by Communism. I remembered Georgi, so full of political passion, who had gone off to fight and die in the mountains. Perhaps they connected me to him.

When the secretary finally appeared, I took the initiative. Why had I been summoned here? I was not a Party member; I had done nothing wrong. With the slightest hand gesture, the Secretary dismissed this protest, as though he had heard it a thousand times. More likely he was dismissing its naiveté. Whether one was a member or not, the Party controlled everything and everyone.

He settled behind his desk and opened a folder. "We are quite pleased with your record since you opposed the Nazis," he said. He referred to a paper in the folder, which I assumed was a clipping of the letter I had written to the newspaper criticizing German presence in Romania during the war. The file was thick, and I got the instant impression that my whole life laid before him, chronicled by the police and by government informers.

"However, your parents and your background . . . are not ideologically sound." His expression registered the import of that fact. A large nose dominated his round face. A thick shock of hair stood from the top of his head. I had seen his picture many times in the newspaper. His name was Nicolae Ceausescu. He had once been a shoemaker, but had risen quickly to prominence by his fanatical pursuit of Party interests. He would one day be Romania's president. In 1950 he was already a man of considerable power who was pointing out this flaw in my background to remind me that if I did not stay in his good graces, he would be forced to crush me. That blunt reality was the common assumption of life in Communist Romania.

I gave no outward reaction to this implied threat, but I well knew that many people had been punished for lesser offenses. And, of course, I had no way to defend myself against such a charge.

"But I have not called you here to discuss that, rather to open the door of opportunity." He showed a weak smile that seemed to invite my gratitude. "We would like you to take charge of the Communist Youth newspaper, to edit it, to build it in size and influence. This is a wonderful opportunity for you."

He was right on that score; it was a wonderful opportunity. The Romanian Communist government was young and still developing. Dramatic career advancement could come overnight. The swift rise of my friend Emil was proof enough of that. Of course, I too had once nourished political ambitions.

The official Party newspaper, *Scanteia* (The Sparkle) was an important organ of the government, its editor a man of considerable influence. Editing the Communist Youth paper, *Scanteia Tineretului*, (The Sparkle Youth), could be a stepping stone to a bright career.

A small part of me was flattered by the offer. I did have a reputation as an intellectual and a good writer. My brief career as student government president had shown my interest in politics. Perhaps having friends that were staunch Party loyalists also suggested that I might be a likely candidate for the position.

Still, I needed no time to consider the offer. I had thought my way through this moment many years ago. My answer was brief and to the point, diplomacy never being my strong point. "I cannot undertake the assignment because I do not share your ideology. Besides, I do not like foreign boots on my country's soil."

Perhaps a more rational man would have taken the offer, would have adapted to the political reality of the moment. But, I did not hesitate in my refusal, because I had a fundamental dislike for any form of indoctrination or regimentation. For the rest of my life, that quality would remain a strong part of my personality. The Soviet occupation of my country at that time was loathsome to me, as it was for most Romanians. It echoed back to German occupation during the war. The Communist ideology was as unpalatable as that of the Nazis. I had witnessed how both governments corrupted society and brutalized the population. I did not want to be a part of this government.

Secretary Ceausescu's expression pinched with annoyance. He was not a man to have his wishes opposed. He had been murderously ruthless in leading the collectivization of agriculture. One head-strong student was but a mosquito in the path of the Party's advance.

"Sometimes when we act too quickly we make foolish decisions," he said. "When you have been given time to think, perhaps you will reach a different conclusion."

I was led to another office, given food and bedding and kept there for three days, to "reflect upon my decision." But my reflections were all one-sided. Aside from my ideological objections to the Secretary's offer, I had firmly determined to leave the country and reunite with my parents in Canada. After three days, I reaffirmed my refusal and was released.

I fully expected some repercussion but certainly not what occurred. Several evenings later the knock came at my door. Two security men in uniform waited there to greet me. "Come along now, quickly," they snapped.

For several months a sweet girl named Puica had been living with me, but she was not home now. I imagined her returning that night to an empty apartment, wondering and worrying day after day why I did not show up. At this point I had not yet made the connection to my refusal to accept Ceausescu's offer. Perhaps something I said or did at the university had precipitated this trouble. Perhaps my "ideologically unsound family." It could have been many things. I could not guess how long I would be detained. "Arrested," I scribbled hastily on a scrap of paper for Puica's benefit. Then, I grabbed up a few items, including the potassium cyanide capsule from my desk drawer, and was led away.

They delivered me to the office of state security, in the same building where two short years earlier I had visited the office of my friend Emil, seeking a passport to leave the country. That coincidence flashed through my mind. I had already shifted into an altered mental state, somewhere between fear, denial, and numbness.

For several days I languished in a cell, awaiting my meeting with the review committee. The whole process was calculated to frighten, and it did. But I would not allow myself to believe the truth of what was happening, at least would not allow myself to confront it. Namely, that I had been arrested and was heading to prison.

Eventually, I was taken before the committee. This was in no sense a trial, no attempt to sort through my case. The papers in my file told them that this was Mark Iutcovich, "Enemy of the People," and so they knew to sentence me to "Administrative Re-education." No term of imprisonment was announced. Perhaps it was too obvious to the committee to need mentioning—The prisoner would be imprisoned for as long as it took to accomplish his re-education. The following day a train took a group of us to Tulcea, where we were put on a boat.

Below Tulcea the Danube River branches into three broad waterways which wind through a delta to the Black Sea. It is a land of lagoons, marshes, and swampy islands, a miasmic place of mud and water, mosquitos, and disease. Here, on a long and desolate peninsula, was located the prison camp called Pereprava. A jagged scar of barbed wire fencing and guard towers enclosed some 300 acres. Several squat buildings and long rows of mud brick barracks gave the place a crude military appearance. This was one outpost in the Land of the Disappeared, one camp of many in the Romanian gulag.

An eerie calm hung over the place the day I arrived. The men were working outside the camp. I would not meet them until late at night when they returned. At the barracks where I was assigned, a rough-looking fellow introduced himself as the head prisoner. "This is my barracks," he announced gruffly. "Follow my rules and there won't be trouble." He indicated a space on a wooden shelf that would be my sleeping spot. A waif-like teenage boy handed me a blanket. Long rows of shelves, two tiers high, extended down both sides of the barracks. Here the prisoners slept, packed in like sardines.

Then my prisoner boss, whom I would later learn was serving 25 years for murder, went over camp procedures and his rules. Up at 3 a.m., breakfast and roll call, then out to work until about 10 p.m. Political prisoners could send and receive mail once a month. Criminals had unlimited mail privileges. You would be fed, but other than that everything had to come from the outside, such as clothing or cigarettes. To stay in his good graces, he expected regular gifts and cigarettes.

It was nearly 11 p.m. when the prisoners returned from their day's labor. I watched warily from my spot on the sleeping shelf. Hundreds dragged themselves in to fill the barracks. You would not have thought the place could hold so many. They were wet and muddy, incredibly exhausted. The place came alive with their smells and sounds—the smells of sweat, the sounds of weary bodies moving mechanically through the motions of retiring. There was no socializing nor ceremony. Most slid quickly into their narrow space on the shelf, a few smoked cigarettes before turning in. The head prisoner, I noticed, who had a bed in the corner, shared it with the boy who had given me my blanket.

There was little acknowledgement of me, a new prisoner on the scene. In short order, I was tightly sandwiched between two warm bodies, the room was dark and buzzed with snoring. I was more frightened than I had ever been in my life. Would this place eat me up? Would I be here for the rest of my life? I wormed my hand into my coat pocket and wrapped it around the cyanide capsule. There was a great comfort in knowing that I could end my life quickly if things got unbearable. Odd that my most valued possession, my darkest secret, was that I possessed the means to kill myself.

* * *

"Get up! Get up!" The head prisoner yelled us awake at 3 a.m. Hundreds of bodies wormed their weary limbs off of the shelves. They dressed, rolled up their blankets, and shuffled off to the latrine. I noticed that a few men had not emerged from their shelves. The head prisoner detailed a work crew to carry them away. They had died in the night.

Prisoners filed past a cook house. I had been given a small tin pot and cup. Into these went hot soup and ersatz coffee, accompanied by a hunk of bread. The soup was a thin, grainy brew that felt warm going down but upset my stomach. I would later swear off of it altogether.

A bedraggled army of men presented themselves for roll call at 4 a.m. Flood lights etched their ranks from the darkness. Their lines extended beyond my sight along the rows of barracks. Later I would learn that nearly 10,000 men resided here, mostly political prisoners. They came from all walks of life—farmers, workers, engineers, professors, students, politicians. Many of them were middle aged or older, men who had held responsible positions in society, but had been less than enthusiastic in their embrace of the new political faith. I kept wondering if I would see someone I knew, someone who had occupied a lectern at the university or whose photo had appeared in the newspaper. I never did. Or, they were unrecognizable.

Here they blended together in one forlorn mass. The camp had no uniforms. Men wore the clothes that had been on their backs when they were arrested or whatever they had received from the outside. But hard labor had worn a threadbare sameness to their clothing. The drudgery of this existence had stamped all their faces with the same vacancy.

After roll call, we were assigned to different work groups and marched off into the night. By the time we arrived at the work site several miles away, dawn had broken on the mist-shrouded shores of the peninsula. It revealed a long earthen wall under construction. The men fell automatically into the routine they knew only too well. Working with shovels and wheelbarrows, they dug dirt and piled it onto the wall. Some set to work along the muddy shore. I waded with others into waist-deep water to dredge mud from the bottom. We filled wheelbarrows that were carted away and added to the wall, along with reinforcing layers of reeds.

I remember looking up numerous times on that first day to watch the men laboring and see load after load of dirt and mud dumped onto the wall. Ostensibly the work of the camp was to construct a dike to protect the peninsula from the delta's periodic floods. But the project looked so huge and our efforts so feeble that I imagined it would take generations of men to complete. I feared that I would be on hand to greet the next generation of prisoners brought into the camp. I feared that I was looking at the rest of my life.

In reality, the dike would serve little useful purpose, if and when it ever got finished. The real mission of the camp was to deal with social misfits, to re-fashion these men in the Communist mold. Hard labor would either completely extinguish the spark of individualism or dampen it enough with the threat of future punishment, thus "Re-educating" us.

The camp philosophy was to extract as much work as possible from the prisoners, at minimal cost. In that respect it followed the Russian more than the German model. Here there was no systematic intent to exterminate, rather it was simply an indifference to a prisoner's survival. The German approach killed the "unwanted" quickly; the Russian / Romanian approach drew out their suffering interminably before killing them. At Pereprava, minimal basic needs were met, and beyond that . . . well, a prisoner's death solved the re-education problem as neatly as a sincere political conversion.

When I dragged myself, bone tired, from the water after that first day, some of the men stopped on shore to strip off their clothing. Fastened to their chests and legs and groins were huge leeches. I quickly tore off my clothes and found nearly a dozen. They were Horse Leeches, five inches long and swollen with my blood. They could only be safely removed with the application of salt. Of course, salt was not provided, but had to be acquired from the outside. Salt was high on my list of requests in the first letter I mailed from the camp.

I was so totally exhausted and depressed after that first day that I collapsed onto my shelf and felt for my cyanide capsule among my belongings. "It is there if I need it," I repeated to myself, and I came very close to using it that first night. But, I was too utterly exhausted to do anything but sleep. Nothing, I would quickly learn, took such a powerful grip on me at Pereprava as exhaustion—complete, absolute weariness of body and mind. Combined with the most basic animalistic impulse for survival, exhaustion would drain all higher concerns from my existence.

* * *

To describe one day of my existence would be to describe hundreds. The weather changed, new prisoners arrived, others died. The numbing treatment and routine remained a constant. Bit by bit I sank to an animal-like existence. It annoys me now to read romanticized accounts of the gulag experience of others. My ordeal did not bond me in friendship with other prisoners. I did not take time to philosophize about politics or life. Everything I did was aimed first at survival, and then at ameliorating my suffering, to whatever extent that could be managed.

Sundays we were given half a day off. Prisoners bathed, washed clothes, and once a month sent or received mail. The first letter I wrote went to a friend of my parents named Roga. I had resolved not to tell my parents of my imprisonment. The news would have killed my mother. Salt was high on my list of requests, but also cigarettes, one of the few pleasures allowed in the camp and also the standard currency. If you wanted any favors, the payment was in cigarettes.

I did not have many correspondents. For my friends who were Communists, the receipt of a letter from an Enemy of the People, would have been hazardous. So, I did not write to Silviu, who had gotten a good job in communications. However, I did write to Ion, then an army officer. He proved a loyal friend, regularly sending me cigarettes.

And I wrote to Puica. In that strange short-hand used by those who lived under Communism, used by those who assumed that prying eyes read every thought they committed to paper, I explained. I said I loved her and asked for cigarettes. In truth, my thoughts of her were bittersweet. In this hell, I did not want to love or long for anyone. I did not want to feel. Attachment caused pain. However, whenever I received cigarettes from Puica, I imagined her dear face and kissed it. Love was such a flimsy crutch in Pereprava, but cigarettes were cigarettes.

Packages had always been opened when I received them. The guards examined their contents and often helped themselves to anything they wanted. But what a pleasure to find a carton of Plugars, the cheap and strong Romanian cigarettes, or to receive a toothbrush, some candy, or a warm hat.

A few packs of cigarettes went to the head prisoner, who held onto the rest for safe keeping. A cigarette to the prisoner who cleaned the barracks assured that your possessions would not be stolen. A cigarette would get your boots cleaned. Three cigarettes to the men in the mess hall and they would heat water for you to bathe with on Sunday. Fortunately, the regular supply of cigarettes I received from outside allowed me to indulge in these simple safeguards and pleasures.

One particular Sunday stands out vividly in my memory. In theory, prisoners were allowed visits once a year. Usually these did not happen. Visitors were not allowed to come to Pereprava. Instead, prisoners were taken off to see their loved ones.

One day, I was notified that I would be taken to Tulcea where someone would be permitted to visit with me. I wrote with great excitement to Puica to meet me there. If memory serves me correctly, I was the only prisoner loaded onto the boat that day. What a mix of emotion filled me as we chugged our way through the delta waters. How desperately I wanted to leave Pereprava for good.

Puica was waiting when the boat pulled up to the dock in Tulcea. "Go ahead." The guard gestured for me to get off. I climbed ashore and gave Puica a hug and a kiss. We sat on the ground for about half an hour. She told me gossipy things about some friends. I told her that I was working very hard. I think she was wary of what to say. The guard couldn't hear us, but what could you say to a man who was in the gulag? A man who might spend the rest of his life in forced labor? Be of good cheer? Everything will be all right?

When the guard said it was time to leave, Puica gave me a small bundle of cigarettes, clothing, and food. I stood at the stern of the boat looking back at her until she disappeared from view.

* * *

Sunday afternoons were a much appreciated respite from our labors. But come the dark of Monday morning and we once again marched to our work. The cooler times of the day brought with them relentless swarms of mosquitoes, black clouds of them swarming around your face and any exposed skin, eager to draw their share of blood before the leeches. At night, they were merciless. In fact, mosquitoes were one of the principal forms of punishment for disruptive prisoners.

Prisoners to be punished were stripped naked and put into a cage of barbed wire, about three feet by four feet. Several of them stood at each end of the compound. A few hours at the mercy of the blood-sucking insects was usually enough to have them yelling for release and promising cooperation. If they were kept in over night, their screams went on through much of the night.

But a worse threat from mosquitoes was malaria. I had contracted it as a child and was thus immune. It was rampant in the camp, and there was no medical treatment. Its victims looked like the walking dead. They suffered the shakes and fevers, and wasted away. They dropped dead while working or lay lifeless on their shelf at morning wakeup. A work crew came and carted away their lifeless corpse, another victim of the gulag.

Winter came on quickly and did little to change our routine. We had our morning roll call, then breakfast. I had sworn off soup by this time. Though it was warm, it fattened the body without nourishing it. It was composed largely of a type of pea, usually fed to animals, that had been foraged from the countryside. It was a harsh concoction that made some sick. I routinely traded my soup for bread. For much of the first two years, I survived almost solely on bread. I would eat a small portion at breakfast, then throughout the day suck on pieces held in my mouth like chewing tobacco.

For about five months of the year Romania is blasted by bitter winds sweeping in from southern Russia. Until the waters of the delta froze, we worked in the water, fighting the cold and its painful effects. But the Danube is usually ice bound three months of the year. We spent those frigid months cutting reeds that would later be used to reinforce the mud construction of the dike.

The cold was brutal, frostbite a common affliction. No clothing, coats, hats, or gloves were supplied to the prisoners. Some had them and some did not. The criminals in camp, who had unlimited mail privileges, would have clothing mailed to them, which they could then trade to the political prisoners for cigarettes or favors. An enterprising criminal could have a bevy of servants attending to many of his chores.

One bitter cold day we were working on ice, cutting and stacking reeds when we heard a shout. A prisoner had broken through the ice and plunged into the frigid water below. We hurried to pull him out. Soaking wet, stunned by his cold bath, he staggered away, and sat on the ground. There was nothing we could do for him. Everyone realized that. As I continued work, I glanced at him from time to time. He stood up once and marched stiffly about, then sat down again. He rubbed his arms. He made no movement after that. My last image of him—the unnatural, stiffened angle of his limbs, indicating that his body was now a block of ice.

Most of the time while I was in Pereprava, my complete awareness was consumed by weariness, hunger, and work. This was probably good. I took less notice of time. Painful thoughts found less of a foothold in my brain. But, sometimes, an occurrence, such as the freezing prisoner, awakened a self-awareness and plunged me into deep despondency.

I had been so exhausted and cold myself that I had not cared that another prisoner died. Prisoners died all the time. I did not agonize over the tragic loss of a human life. What purpose would it have served? Stay warm, suck the last bit of nourishment from the wad of bread in my mouth, sleep—only the most elemental concerns were strong enough to register in my consciousness.

"Look at me," I would think, during such moments. "What have I been reduced to? Am I still a human being?" Because I did not know the length of my sentence, I also did not know whether I had to bear up to this for another month, another year, or the rest of a wretched life.

Early in my sentence, I nurtured an anger over the turn of events that had landed me in this hell. I was angry at the Americans for not saving me, angry at Roosevelt and Churchill and all the Allies for selling out Romania at Yalta, where the post-war division of Europe had been decided. The Allies had divided Europe just as the Germans had done, and when the Soviet Union had moved to make the countries of Eastern Europe its client states, the West had done nothing. I hated everyone and everything remotely responsible for Romania's current circumstances and for my own.

But, deep into my sentence, that hatred had dissipated, and I missed it. It had been a strong, vitalizing emotion, something to which to cling, from which to take strength. Now it too was gone, along with other human emotions. Sometimes at night, waiting for sleep on my shelf, I would search for that hatred. What had been my exact thoughts about the Allies? What words had I used to curse them? How had it felt to care so passionately about something? Had my muscles tightened? my pulse quickened? I murmured curses, but they were lifeless. I no longer had the ability or the energy to connect with hatred.

And so, seconds away from a dead sleep, my thinking touched on the cyanide capsule. I could picture it in exact detail, its appearance, its paper wrapper, its safe hiding place among my clothing. Then it struck me—with a shock—that the capsule aroused no emotion in me whatsoever. My comforting attachment to my means of death had also abandoned me, like everything else. Once I had embraced that pill with such conviction, knowing that I possessed the will to use it if I chose. Now . . . what was the fuss? I was hungry and wanted to eat, cold and wanted warmth, weary beyond all measure and only wanted to sleep. I wanted, for some unaccountable reason, to keep going, to survive.

7
Desire to Survive

Snow whipped the yard where we stood for roll call. Even though I had not one whit of religious sentiment, I blessed dear Roga for having recently sent me a pair of warm gloves. Many of the prisoners had to make do with tattered old gloves or ones fashioned from rags. Some prisoners did not hold up well in winter, the old and those made weak by hunger and disease. The shivers of malaria gave way to the shivers of cold.

It is hard to convey the commanding presence of coldness in our lives. I had thought weariness was such a monster, stealing my thoughts, mindlessly consuming my life. Cold could be worse. It was more insistent, more immediately threatening. Months would pass without warmth ever once thawing the ice that had settled in my joints and muscles. The toll of the dead rose dramatically in winter.

Our barracks was not heated, and even though bodies so closely packed for sleeping generate their own warmth, we still slept in coats, hats, and gloves. The vapor of our breathing hung in the air like fog. Coughing and hacking punctuated the night. In the morning, half a dozen or more might not rise from sleep. Prisoners carried them away to what I imagined to be some massive common grave outside the camp, the true monument to our work in this place.

The relatives and friends of those who died would never know what became of them. Their loved one would simply never return from prison. There would be no official statement. And certainly, one never inquired about such things. More than dying, I dreaded that, slipping away into anonymous death. My parents, who were still unaware of my imprisonment, would eventually learn from my correspondents that I had stopped writing letters. Those are all the details they would have—Mark was imprisoned; he wrote for awhile and then stopped. It would be as enigmatic a loss as my grandmother disappearing from the train while fleeing the Nazi advance in Bessarabia. I had no doubt that the loss of a third son under such circumstances would kill my dear parents.

Flames danced in my head as I awaited roll call. Sometimes in winter we built a bonfire at the work site, and indulgent guards allowed us to briefly cluster around its warmth. I was daydreaming about that possibility when one of the guards yelled, "Is anyone here a civil engineer?" No one responded. "An engineer who knows surveying," he added. My hand shot up. What was I doing? I was not an engineer and knew nothing about surveying. Still, I imagined it would be better work than digging mud and cutting reeds.

I was taken to the prisoner in charge of engineering, a fellow named Stancu, in a small building on the edge of the compound. Several large tables filled the room; men leaned over them working on maps. The room was heated! It made my head spin.

"Where did you receive your schooling?" Stancu asked me.

"University of Bucharest," I said.

He gave me a quizzical look. "I was a professor of engineering at the University and I do not remember you."

When I explained that my training was in sociology not engineering, he slapped his forehead and told me to get out. But I jumped in quickly with the argument that there were no engineers among the prisoners and that I would be a good and eager student. "If in two or three hours I can't learn what I need to know, then send me back."

When he hesitated, I pulled out a pack of cigarettes. "Here. This is a down payment. I will give you cigarettes and food. You will be glad I am here." He finally relented, and I became an engineer.

I was put in charge of a three-man survey crew. Fortunately, some of those men knew what they were doing. Each morning we reported to the engineering building. Here, maps gave a larger perspective to the delta. One showed our peninsula, with the straight line of the dike along one edge. Of the many delta islands indicated on the maps, some had details sketched in and others remained blank outlines.

Each day I would venture out with my crew in the company of a guard to gather coordinates on local features: roads, houses, buildings, settlements. There was nothing so large as a town, but mere clusters of homes, where settlers had carved pastures and fields from the surrounding wilderness. The farmers here had migrated from the mainland to claim small parcels of property, to live and work in peace on ground they could call their own.

Like most of the other guards at the Pereprava, our guard was a local peasant himself, with no political axe to grind. This was just a job for him, and he treated us decently. If we finished our assigned work early, he would allow us time to rest. If, while surveying, we came upon an orchard, he turned his back while we gathered fruit. When we carried such harvests back to camp, he smuggled them through the gate, then returned them to us inside.

The head prisoner in my barracks got his share of the booty. Some I gave away and some I used as a new form of currency to acquire favors. Cigarettes and items acquired from the outside had always been our form of money to purchase favors or to exchange for other items. I found that apples also served this purpose.

I exalted in my new-found status. I had regained a small measure of control over my life. Even so small a triumph as having cigarettes or a few apples to gain protection or buy a favor, gave me a feeling of independence. Helplessness, being totally at the mercy of the system, was a terrible sensation that dropped me to the level of an animal. Each small increase in my ability to influence circumstances made me feel more like a human being.

When the map of peninsula had been pretty much filled in, we took rowboats to nearby islands to continue our survey. We drew in roads and plotted the location of homes and farms. When these islands too had been surveyed, we rode a large motor launch to more distant islands. The rich land of the islands had attracted numerous settlements, but many did not appear on the maps.

It must have been a curious sight, this prisoner survey crew, because people living in the area where we were working would come out to watch us work. They stood off a ways and eyed us with suspicion. Some came right up and asked what we were up to. "Surveying, making maps," we told them. Word spread. One day as we surveyed along the edge of a village, a farmer appeared. For some time, he watched us closely, then approached.

"It would hurt nothing to move your stake over to here," he suggested to me, indicating a spot several feet away. I did not immediately grasp his motive in this, but merely responded that such a thing would be impossible since we needed an accurate survey. When he persisted, I said that the guard and the other members of the crew would never allow it. The farmer went away but returned shortly with a sausage, an offering to put us in a more obliging mood. We moved the stake.

The peasants on these islands had seen a survey crew but smelled a rat. Their comparative isolation had protected them thus far from the grasping hands of government nationalization and agricultural collectivization. Now, in this survey, they realized that the government would know the exact extent of their properties. And they were right. Our survey plotted the location of farms, buildings, pastures, fields, orchards, vineyards, every improvement and thing of value. It would be very much to their advantage if government records showed them owning less land, smaller orchards, and having fewer acres under cultivation.

Suddenly, I and my crew had considerable power, and these peasants came to court our favor as though we were roving potentates. This one brought grapes, this one a pot of hot stew. These barns need not appear on the survey; this creek could be situated a hundred meters to the west.

A woman showed up at one location, explaining that she was a widow who worked very hard to get by. She walked with us around the perimeter of her meager farm. She kept the animals here, pastured them there, had a small garden in back. She wished for our survey to show her farm to be even smaller than it was.

I confess to fighting back a lustful desire at that moment. She wanted a large favor, I was in a position to grant it, and I had not been with a woman in over two years. Nor had any moral compunction survived to stand in my way. Instead, I worried about overstepping my bounds as a prisoner and losing this choice work assignment.

I directed her to the guard. If she slept with him, I suggested, he would most likely grant her request. She did. We altered our survey data. For a few weeks, as we continued to survey that area, the two of them continued their arrangement. While the guard was distracted with her, we were free to sleep or eat.

Although we tried to keep secret just how good we had it on the survey crew, some figured it out and pleaded to join us. When I thought I could get away with it, I put on extra men, four or five of us would labor to invent this bogus survey. However, I worried about the consequences if too many people knew of this arrangement, and camp officials started asking questions. But, they seemed to be unaware of what went on outside the camp, or if they knew, seemed not to care.

Meanwhile, all of our faulty survey data were being drawn onto the maps of the delta. Some days I sat in the engineering office with Stancu and his draftsmen, meticulously transferring my raw data onto the maps. The widow's farm was drawn on the map at half its actual size. For one spicy sausage, another farmer had completely removed his orchard from the map.

How carefully we labored to create this typical Communistic record of reality. I had seen this false reality emerge first at the university, where the past was rewritten to reflect political purpose. History, facts, reality, were denied, ignored, reinterpreted to fit a political agenda. The curriculum was altered to give everything a Marxist slant. Even a student's grades might better reflect his Party loyalty than his accomplishments in the classroom.

This was the common smoke and mirrors game of Communism. At the university, I had learned what Marxist dribble was expected on tests and papers, and therefore I provided that for the professor, simply to get by, to survive in the academic environment.

Surveying was the same game. Deep inside, I still resented the nationalization of my family property. I sympathized with these peasants, trying to preserve a few scraps of their property and their independent way of life. So, even though our mission was to portray the physical reality of islands, our personal agenda distorted that reality. I exalted at even so small a victory over the system of the gulag that was trying to break me down. This minor bit of rebellion on my part served the dual purpose of nurturing both my body and my spirit.

* * *

In March 1953, I was working on my third year in Pereprava.

"I have some news for you men." The tone of the guard's voice made this sound important. The survey crew stopped its work and gave him its full attention. "I saw it in the newspaper yesterday," he said. "Stalin is dead."

A shock wave passed through all of us as we absorbed the news and its implications. But that was quickly replaced by joy. We gave a cheer and were all smiles.

"Maybe things will go different now," the guard offered. He seemed nearly as pleased with the news as we were.

Maybe they will, we all agreed. After all, Stalin was the great architect of Communism's repressive reign. With him out of the way, the situation in Eastern Europe might change dramatically. A move by the West to break the Soviet grip? Soviet troops out of Romania? Could it happen?

A different government in Bucharest? Who could foretell the final repercussions of this monster's death?

Of course, amid all those fanciful thoughts, the one that came to the front was the chance of our release from Pereprava. Government policy might change. They might realize the insanity of the gulag. The gates might fly open. We might be sent home. It was too sweet to contemplate. For weeks after this news, daydreams of freedom buoyed my spirits.

However, weeks went by, spring turned to summer, and nothing changed. Even when the initial euphoria had given way to a more rational consideration of the possibilities, I still clung to a thread of hope that political change would lead to early release. But slowly, begrudgingly, I let go of that hope as well.

Autumn arrived, and I was coming up on the third anniversary of my imprisonment. Some of the survey work now took us to distant islands. We would stay there for two or three days, living in an abandoned house or with a peasant family. We ate heartily and were treated well on these occasions. Now and then, women made sexual advances to me or my crew. But I always refused and insisted that my men do likewise. Let the guard indulge in those pleasures.

This was not from prudishness or lack of interest on my part, but because I still worried about jeopardizing this privileged assignment that we all enjoyed. I was increasingly anxious that camp officials would get wind of the gifts we had been bringing back to the camp and might question us about how we had acquired them. They might take a closer look at some of the survey information. So, we took our pleasure in the nourishing food and the civil treatment of those good people and continued with our work, hoping this fortunate assignment would last.

There came one chilly morning that autumn when a guard ordered me to stay behind at the prison when my crew went out to work. This was not a good sign, I quickly concluded, and braced myself for some reprimand. Had they learned of our bogus survey? Had some peasant complained? some prisoner informed?

I was taken to the camp office, and there a glum-faced guard announced very nonchalantly, "You are being released. Get your things. The boat is leaving shortly."

Released? Leaving? My head swam with disbelief and excitement. I grabbed my meager possessions from the barracks. There was only one individual to whom I wished to bid farewell, the head engineer, Stancu.

"Congratulations," he said with genuine but restrained good will. My good fortune was a reminder that he would remain here. "Do me a favor," he said. "My family lives in Bucharest. Go there and tell my wife that I am well. Tell her to send cigarettes. And a wool sweater would be nice." I assured him that I would visit her.

We said goodbye, and shortly I was on a motor launch chugging my way out of the delta.

* * *

What a great surprise it was for dear Puica to see my face at the door. What a great joy for me to receive her kisses and spend that first night in a real bed with her. I was reborn, drunk with my regained freedom. I savored anew each small joy of life: a meal with friends, a walk in the park, moments of privacy. Pereprava and all its misery lay behind me.

But Puica wanted to hear all about my ordeal, details, names, stories, horrors. The worst of the details mesmerized her most, like a child fascinated by scary stories. I encountered the same keen curiosity from my neighbors and old friends when they saw me again. Their expression changed, their voice took on a different tone when they broached the subject. "What happened there? What was it like?"

The gulag had already become a fixture in our national consciousness. So many people had relatives, friends, or acquaintances who had been taken there. So many whispered-portrayals of the camps circulated that they had become something of a collective nightmare. Right here in our own country there existed this invisible, monstrous land, and at any moment, any one might be snatched from family and friends and transported there.

I could tell none of this to my parents when I wrote to them for the first time in three years. I did not want them to worry for my safety, and of course, one did not commit such things to paper. So I said only that I had been very busy. I'm sure they suspected what had really happened.

My parents had continued to send me $100 a month for all that time. It had been accumulating in an account at the British embassy. I could not visit there to claim my money. A visit to any foreign embassy would have earned me a quick return trip to the gulag. But the embassy handled a number of such arrangements and was adept at the cloak and dagger game of life inside Romania.

Without using my name, I wrote to the embassy with enough information to establish my identity. They then sent me a check of my accumulated wealth. How sweet to be free once again and to have about $3,600, a modest fortune in 1953 Romania.

I wrote to Roga, who lived in Galatz, and thanked him most profusely for helping to sustain me over the past three years with his letters and packages. I hoped to find some way to repay his kindness.

As I had promised, I also visited Stancu's wife. It felt like a final thread linking me to Pereprava, that I needed to cut before I could finally appreciate my freedom. She was a dignified woman, living in half of a small apartment. A few pieces of art hinted at the more comfortable life she had once enjoyed as a professor's wife. I gave her a brief account of my work with her husband, assured her that he was in good health, and passed along his requests. She seemed to take hope from the fact that I had been released after three years.

* * *

What stands out strongest in my memory from this time was my undiminished desire to leave Romania. I applied for a passport, but received no response. There were lawyers one could resort to, but they were con men, more intent on separating you from your money than from your homeland.

Yet there was reason for some optimism. Some people were being given passports. A few Jews were allowed to emigrate to Israel. At one point I thought I might fabricate papers to prove I was a Jew. Instead, I nurtured the faint hope that eventually, the government would decide that there was no reason to keep such a malcontent as Mark Iutcovich in the country, and they would grant me a passport.

Puica and I had a few more blissful months together in that one crowded room of my old apartment. She was a physician and worked long hours. We ate in restaurants, and I bought her presents—a blouse or a pair of shoes picked up on the black market. These were real treasures in those days. I remember a friend living with us for awhile. He had to sleep on several chairs pushed together for a makeshift bed. Housing was so critically short that one didn't complain about such arrangements. In fact, most everything was in short supply.

This tranquil period had to come to an end. I had been emotionally buoyed by my regained freedom and by having a considerable reserve of cash. But both of those were dwindling. After a few months, Puica moved out. She shared an apartment with another woman. Several times over the next year, we tried to get together again, without success.

Thinking about it now, I don't believe I have ever left any of the women who have come into my life; they always left me. I may well have given them ample cause to leave, but they did the leaving. I was always freer with my resources than with myself, buying them gifts, taking them to good restaurants, loaning money. My father always said that money is the cheapest commodity. If it can solve problems or save you headaches, spend it freely. Giving of yourself, on the other hand, is more expensive.

This was always my approach to relationships. It was not an intentional strategy that I plotted, but a natural outgrowth of my personality. I won't speculate about the psychological roots of that personality trait, but it has defined my relationships with others.

So, I was alone. It had become apparent that I would not be leaving the country any time soon. I began to apply for work and seek out freelance translation assignments again, anything to have a dribble of income to sustain me. It represented an enormous shift in my thinking, but I began to think of living a life in Communist Romania. It felt very much like I had been knocked down and trampled by the new Romania. I had stood back up, dusted myself off, gotten my bearings, and now needed to strike off in a new direction. It appeared as though my future would be, in Romania.

One day, shortly after Puica had moved out that first time, I was rearranging clothes in a dresser drawer and came upon the trousers I had worn in Pereprava. Oh, my. There in my hand lay the discolored wrapper holding my cyanide pill. I folded back the dirty paper and stared at that tiny glass capsule. How small and insignificant it looked. How odd that it had once been my most valued possession. I carried it outside, placed it on the sidewalk, and crushed it with my shoe.

8
Life in the Peoples' Republic

A package arrived from my parents in Canada, always a cause for excitement. I opened it in my room and laid out the contents on the table. Some canned goods. These were a much appreciated supplement to my meager diet. Packets of Nescafé coffee. I spread them out to make the quantity seem even greater than it was. Some of these I would savor myself, but most I would sell. I could not afford to consume such luxuries too often. Three pairs of nylon stockings. What prizes. Two I would sell, and one would be a present to a lady friend; it would delight her beyond all measure and raise me high in her esteem.

Lining the bottom of the box was a length of fine woolen material. I had specifically requested it from my parents. Also, a plaid scarf. Good as gold on the black market. I already had a customer for the material. I wrapped it in newspaper, threw on my coat and headed to his apartment.

Once again, I found myself working as a black marketeer, an "economic saboteur." Months had gone by since my release from Pereprava, and I still had no job. I had applied for many but not been hired. I suspected that the state wanted to take its time with me, see if I behaved myself. In six months, a year—they were very patient—if I had not caused trouble, I would find work. Until then, I needed to be resourceful.

I still received the $100 a month from my parents, and now also these packages of treasures. The cryptic messages in the letters I exchanged with my parents did not allow us to tell much about our lives, but I imagined them living in considerable comfort with the money they had taken out of Romania. It made me long all the more to be with them in Canada. Why should I be languishing in poverty, unable to find work, when wealth and opportunity awaited me in Canada? Sometimes I fantasized what life would be like for me there, a romantic picture of financial independence, intellectual and professional freedom.

But I was not in Canada, I was in Romania, it was 1954, and I enjoyed none of those items from my fantasy. Earlier that morning I had spent nearly two hours, from 3 a.m. to 5 a.m., standing in line to buy ice for my ice box. Everything was in short supply, almost everything was rationed, and waiting in line for purchases was a fact of life. Staples, such as meat, sugar, and flour, required coupons to purchase. Though I was again doing freelance translating work, I was not formally employed and thus did not receive ration coupons.

Whenever I was living with someone who got coupons from a job, I enjoyed these items. And friends would occasionally have me over for a meal. Produce, in season, was available without coupons, and that made up much of my diet. How many meals of potatoes, onions, and garlic I cooked on my little gas stove, I couldn't imagine. One day potatoes and onions, the next potatoes and garlic, over and over.

I disembarked a bus on the north side of Bucharest, on my way to my black market contact. Before the war, individual shops had lined this street. Shoppers would bustle about, package-laden, as they visited one store and then the other. I recalled a spring day, as a schoolboy, when I had strolled this street and discovered a bakery where I bought a cherry torte, and had felt very cosmopolitan to be discovering Bucharest on my own.

The row of shops had now been replaced by a couple of state-run stores. A line stretched from one of them. To reassure those waiting in line, a loud speaker mounted on a building blared economic news; some factory or collective farm had exceeded its production quota. What a farce. Who was fooled by these feeble attempts to hide the economic reality of Communism beneath layer upon layer of propaganda? The outside world, who could not trade goods or currency with any Communist country? The citizens, who were rationed nearly every commodity? Or, the Communist leaders, comfortable in their villas and gladdened by the fantasy reports of increased production?

What a strange impression the scene has left on my memory. Here I was, an unrepentant, bourgeois capitalist, ex-convict, on a black-market mission for my financial survival, confronting the evidence of economic hardship and hearing the typical government propaganda of economic progress. And lurking in my memory was the simple childhood pleasure of eating a torte. A mind tuned to such ironies, as mine seemed to be, had ample opportunity to discover them in those days.

When I arrived at the apartment of a man named Dimitri, he was delighted to buy the cloth. There was just over three meters, enough to make a man's suit, for which he paid me 1,000 leis. That was the equivalent of about a month's wages for a factory worker. I also showed Dimitri the plaid scarf I had received. He would put out the word, he said.

That was how the black market worked. "Economic sabotage," was rampant and yet considered a very serious crime. So, it took place behind the scenes, underground. Dimitri would let some of his contacts know that a scarf was for sale. I would also tell a few friends that a scarf was available. Eventually, someone would get back to me that they knew of a person in need of a scarf. Money would change hands, and their neck would be warmer that winter. Cumbersome perhaps, and yet a system that filled some of the yawning gaps in the controlled economy.

I don't remember what I did with my sudden wealth on that occasion, but usually I would splurge. Once a month, when I received the check from my parents, I treated myself to a restaurant meal, often with a girlfriend. You could still eat in restaurants without ration coupons. Though this was a considerable luxury for me, it was one treat I allowed myself. What else did I have to brighten my existence? What did I have to offer these women beyond my affection? An occasional gift from the West, a monthly meal?

Puica continued to come back into my life from time to time. She still lived with a girlfriend when she wasn't with me. She would move back to my room, and things would be fine for a few months, then she would leave again. Move in, move out. Whatever stood between us always resurfaced to drive us apart. Maybe it was that she wanted a future, wanted to be able to plan for marriage and children—all those normal concerns—and my mind simply would not focus very far beyond the moment. Eventually, she stopped returning.

In my defense, I must point out that many shared my attitude of living for the moment. Certainly there were exceptions, individuals who fell in love, married, gave birth, and struck a course in life. But many of us fell under a psychological condition that is hard to define. We did not want to be part of the system; there was no future for us, and so we devised strategies to get by. My goals were always short-term: find a good meal, earn money, have a lover.

My childhood friends Silviu and Ion still lived in Bucharest. Ion was still in the army, still dating Phylicia. I enjoyed their company. We would occasionally meet at a restaurant or visit each other's apartment. They talked about emigrating to Israel and building a life in the new Jewish state. But Ion had been talking of that for years; I did not expect to lose him any time soon.

It was from Ion that I first heard the rumors about Emil. That he had become consumed by the power of his position in State Security, that he beat and tortured people in his office, that he was a complete tool of the worst impulses of the Communist government. Though I knew the government capable of such things, I resisted believing them about Emil. Still, the more I thought about it, the more often I recalled my last meeting with him, and the cold, officious mask he wore that seemed to close out all friendship and humanity, I had to concede the possibility.

Silviu continued working in communications. He visited infrequently, and when he did his nervousness was apparent. He did not speak openly nor stay long. I'm sure he worried about having contact with someone whose official status was still undefined. Given his position, his concerns may have been justified.

The new Romania had taken the lives of four school boys from Braila and shaped them in very different ways.

*   *   *

In 1954 Soviet Premier Nikita Khrushchev began talking about the possibility of peaceful co-existence with the West, but Romanian President Georghiu-Dej remained steadfast in his Stalinist ideals and his complete hostility towards the West. Romanians who had any ties with the West were persecuted. Intellectuals with pro-West sympathies were labeled as "class enemies."

It was during that first year out of Pereprava, when my circumstances were especially bleak, that I received a visit from someone from my past. It was Ileana, the sister of Katty, the woman whose husband had managed our family farm, and with whom I had maintained a long-running affair. "Katty is waiting for you in Greece," Ileana explained. Katty had left her husband and now wanted me to join her. Ileana seemed so delighted to bring me the news, as though with this one stroke she would reunite star-crossed lovers and insure our future happiness.

Ileana herself was about to leave for Greece and was only in Bucharest for a few days awaiting final arrangements. Like Katty, Ileana was Greek and thus allowed to leave the country. I envied her enormously. I would have liked nothing better than to join her in Greece, but I saw no prospect of that. Ileana stayed with me while awaiting her flight out. We cast something of a melancholy mood talking about the old days. Our talk about the future felt strained, as though we put on a face for each other. Things would go better for me in Romania, we agreed. And a bright future awaited her in Greece. We talked, we drank, finding pleasure in these fantasies.

Before she left, we made love. Lying in bed, in her warm embrace, felt wonderfully consoling. Maybe that's why we slept together. Even though I told her to tell Katty that I still loved her and would eventually join her, Ileana knew that such declarations meant nothing, and yet we pretended to believe in them. Going to Greece was beyond my control, and loving, too, required different circumstances. Holding onto each other was what counted to us, whether in bed or in a long-distance, romantic attachment that had no chance of survival.

I corresponded with Katty a few times. Eventually, I received a letter from Ileana saying that Katty had gotten back with her husband and that all three of them were emigrating to Australia. That was the last I heard of them. In my imagination, I picture them managing a vast sheep ranch in their new country.

It was moments such as this—and there were dozens of them—when I became aware of how the emotional core of my life had become so fragmented. Events had scattered my family and friends to the four corners of the globe. Oppression, war, political upheaval, and economic hardship had dispersed them to Argentina, the Soviet Union, Canada, Israel, France, Greece, Australia. Sometimes I felt like the last survivor at a forsaken outpost.

* * *

After more than a year of applying for jobs, I was finally hired as a planificator at a clothing factory. This is a position unknown outside of the Communist world, but in a "planned economy" every enterprise has a planner, someone who determines whether the government's overall plan for economic growth is being followed in the factory and who takes measures to meet the Plan. This was my job and my joke.

Every different item that we manufactured counted for so many points. A certain shirt might equal 300 points, another shirt only 250. Skirts might be 600, pants 750, coats 1500. Points for every conceivable item were set down in a large catalog. At the end of every day, we could tally the points of our production and determine whether we were making sufficient progress towards achieving our plan.

Unlike companies in a capitalist economy who must *sell* their products, and must therefore be concerned with quality, style, and consumer demand, we were only concerned with accumulating points. If the company achieved its point goal, the workers got bonuses; managers got bonuses, awards, and promotions; and the government could boast about Economic Progress. In a sense, my job was to create the illusion of economic progress.

Therefore, we did not hesitate to make winter coats when the weather was warm, or dresses even though we knew the market already had enough dresses for the next two years, or the same pants we had always produced. Accumulating the most points was our only concern. The entire economy functioned in this way.

Romania's first Five-Year Plan for economic growth ended in 1955. It was grandly announced that the country's industrial development had risen to a level nearly three times greater than that of 1938. What great craziness and deception. I still stood in line hours for a piece of ice, still could not buy a loaf of bread, and store shelves were still empty. The black market remained the only place where individual initiative and resourcefulness flourished, providing consumers with those products they really wanted.

I eventually made a connection to an old family friend named Dorscheimer, who sat on the Textile Council, and through him got a planificator job at a larger factory for more pay. I now earned 1,000 leis a month, about $100. My duties were essentially the same. Each morning I met with the foreman and technicians to plan production for the day, then returned to my office to calculate if we would meet the Plan, then make adjustments if necessary. We *always* exceeded the Plan. I was good at juggling numbers and altering production to maximize points. We all got bonuses, and everyone was happy.

Well, almost everyone. The factory director had taken an instant dislike to me, whether because I had been imposed on him from a higher authority or because of personal chemistry, I couldn't say. But he sought opportunities to berate me and undercut my work. After this had continued for months, I felt my mother's wrath stir inside me. Never forgive or forget.

It so happened that the manager was engaged in large scale theft of material and clothing from the factory for sale on the black market. He was certainly not alone in his thievery. In fact, thievery of government goods and services had become pandemic. Right there in the newspapers, next to the glowing accounts of full restaurants, bountiful harvests, and productive factories, were regular reports of economic saboteurs caught by the police. The streetcar that was supposed to be in the repair shop was really in service, the driver pocketing the fares. The Secretary of Agriculture himself made a legal sale of a train load of wood to Czechoslovakia, but then illegally diverted it for sale to Israel, to line his pockets.

From top to bottom, nearly everyone was stealing. Workers pilfered goods, or used company equipment and time to make goods they could sell. Those in authority had grander schemes, such as selling goods to state stores, then buying them back to sell on the black market. Since most workers were paid a monthly salary that only covered their expenses for a week, everyone needed to be resourceful.

A technician visited my office one day and secretively closed the door. The director is planning to fire you, he said. He has been conspiring to make your performance look bad, so that he can justify it. I knew the director was capable of this, and so decided to take action. On a day that I knew he had loaded clothing into his car, I telephoned the police to report a case of economic sabotage. I watched from the window as the Director left work that day. The police greeted him just outside the factory gate. They made him get from the car and open the trunk. He stood there gesturing, spouting excuses. He was arrested, and we shortly had a new director.

It's hard to justify my behavior on that occasion. It's hard to condemn his thievery in the context of the times. But, thanks to my mother, my vindictive streak ran strong and deep. I suppose, too, there was also an element of personal survival involved. My employment and reputation were threatened. I was not about to stand by and let this villain send me back to the land of the unemployed through no fault of my own.

* * *

When I look back on the decade of the 1950's, few landmarks stand out. I was dimly aware of the larger political events playing themselves out on the international scene, at least whatever was reported through the government media.

In 1955 a Four Powers meeting in Geneva to lessen East-West tension ended in failure. In February of 1956 Khrushchev made his famous speech denouncing Stalin. September 1956 saw the Suez Crisis, and October of that year brought the ill-fated Revolution against the Communist government in Hungary. At the universities, where the winds of liberal change found some receptive minds, crackdowns occurred. To a large extent, I was not aware of these things. Overall, very little changed in Romania to suggest that the future would be any different than the present.

* * *

Ion stopped by one day, distressed. Phylicia had gone to Israel to be with her old boyfriend. This was the same boyfriend whose long-ago stint in prison had provided the opportunity for my involvement with Phylicia. But Ion's pain was short-lived. Before long Phylicia's boyfriend died, and Ion too emigrated to Israel to be with her. Ion had been a part of my life since primary school; I knew I would miss him. My old friends continued to disappear, while new faces came and went.

I remember a lovely girl named Marta who lived with me for a while. Although we slept together, she was saving her technical virginity for marriage. When marriage seemed to come no closer for us, she left. And there was the gymnast whom I hired to exercise the workers at the factory. She would visit my office to complain about the violent personality of the man with whom she lived. We talked, commiserated; we became friends, then lovers. We had no illusions about a long-term relationship. Our day-time affair provided her with a pleasant respite from the unpleasantness at home. It filled an emptiness in me and filled several months with pleasure in the late 1950s.

In retrospect that decade had a mood to it, for me at least. Most everything was temporary, ephemeral, and false. I played along, as I had done since the Communists first arrived in my country, but I was not connected to the life around me. It was not part of the traditional world of my youth and not part of the fantasy I imagined for my life when I would leave Romania.

Furthermore, I did not want connections, anything that would tie me to this place. Nothing depressed me more then to imagine I might never leave that country. My whole personality and approach to life was geared to that departure. I could ruin an entire day simply by asking myself the question, "What if it never happens? You never get to leave Romania? What then?

*　*　*

"Do you know who this is?" the phone caller asked, in a tone just mysterious enough to grab my attention. There was no reason I should have recognized the voice after all these years. I had not spoken to this person for over ten years, not since our last, bitter encounter in 1948 when he refused to help me get a passport. But my mind instantly pulled from memory the face of my childhood friend, Emil. I was careful not to speak the name on the phone.

When he said that we had to meet, his voice took on an urgency that suggested something was wrong. Was he in trouble? Was he now coming to me for assistance? What a curious turn of events that would be.

We met in the park across from my apartment building. It was a grey winter day. We were both bundled in coats, though mine was the typical poor quality garment found in the government stores, and Emil's was a tailored, wool coat, an obvious import from the west.

It is hard to describe the mix of emotions I felt when we stood face to face. Thoughts of childhood, of his hearty embrace of Communism, the worst of the rumors that had circulated about his brutality, my own aborted ambition to pursue a political career, and our last angry encounter. We did not shake hands; I do not think either of us even smiled. We simply took a hasty appraisal of each other, and then he spoke.

There was trouble, he said, a shakeup in government. "I may not have my position much longer. So, I wanted to give you this." He handed me a brown envelope. "It's a passport," he explained. "I suggest you use it quickly."

My heart was racing. I needed to take a breath before I could thank him. He wished me luck and then left. Our whole meeting took no more than five minutes. I never saw him again. Not long after that meeting, Emil's mentor Teohari Georgescu was thrown into jail, and Emil lost his job. Many years later I would learn that he had become a professor and a well-respected art historian. Ironically, in the end, two lives which began on the same path but took very different routes, reached similar destinations.

Standing in that chilly Bucharest park, my whole being instantly crystallized around the thought of leaving Romania as soon as possible. I needed a plan. I needed money. My mind spun with details. There was an old family friend living in Bucharest. He had been like family to us when we lived in Braila. He was the only one I could think to turn to. I headed directly for his apartment, told him of the circumstances and asked to borrow 1,000 lei ($100 dollars) for my trip. In that time and place, there were few things more compelling than an opportunity to leave the country, and so he did not hesitate to help me.

Back at my own apartment, I examined the passport for the first time. It was a genuine, Romanian passport, with my photo and the proper stamps. It was really going to happen, I assured myself. I was going to leave Romania.

"I will be traveling to Timosaura for a few days to visit friends," I told my neighbors. I contacted no one, said no goodbyes, whispered not a word of my plan to anyone. The network of government informers extended like a vast spider web throughout the society; I needed to take every precaution.

What would my friends think the next day, the next week, when they found me gone? Mark has disappeared, again. Arrested? They would worry. Anxiety and paranoia would take a firmer grip on their imagination. But that was the way it had to be.

That night I packed a few valuables and some underwear into a briefcase, not wanting to arouse suspicions by carrying luggage. Nervous energy kept me from getting much sleep that night. There was so much to think about, to worry about.

Trying to act casual at the train station the next morning, I naturally felt enormously conspicuous, as though I were giving a bad acting performance to cover my criminal intentions, and it was obvious to everyone. I was sweating. To play it safe, I purchased a ticket to Timisoara, in-country travel that was completely legal without a passport. At Timisoara I would purchase a ticket to Greece.

For the whole, agonizing ride to Timisoara I kept imagining all that could go wrong. What if they discovered that my passport had not been properly issued? What if there was some discrepancy? What if they detained me and made phone calls to learn the truth? Was it possible that Emil had laid a trap for me? I drove myself crazy with worry, trying to keep at bay my worst fear, that I would spend the rest of my life, not in the glorious freedom of the West, but in another hell hole like Pereprava.

At Timisoara I boarded another train without incident heading for Yugoslavia. Now the only hurdle between me and freedom was the border check point. When the train stopped there, all the passengers disembarked to have their papers examined and then board a Yugoslavian train waiting at another siding. As it turned out, I was the very last one in line. It was a sharply cold winter day, and I was shivering. Still, I was certain that my nervousness would alert their suspicions.

But it went off smoothly, a stamp on the passport, and I found myself on a train *outside* of Romania. That's when it hit me. My body began to shake, bringing all my emotions exploding to the surface. For miles and miles, as Romania and my old life slipped behind me, I was lost to uncontrollable crying. The nervous tension of the past 24 hours had brought me to the edge of this precipice, but the release I felt was much deeper than that.

How long I had waited for this moment? Emotionally, I had detached myself from Romania more than a decade ago. So much of my life during that period had simply been marking time, no goals, no lasting attachments, just living for the moment. A few months earlier I had turned 29 years old, and it felt all the world as though I would now be emerging from a protracted adolescence and my real life could begin.

What would I find in Canada? How hard would it be to start over again in life? I was buoyed in my worries by thoughts of my parents. I longed to see them again. They had made the transition. And they waited there to welcome and assist me.

9
Starting Over in the New World

It didn't take long for me to appreciate the different character of life in Greece. From the moment I stepped off the train in Athens, the vitality of the city assaulted me. It bustled with commerce and with a mix of people from many countries. It took this view to better impress upon me the slumber into which Romania had fallen under Communism.

My false passport had been confiscated by the Greek police, so I visited the Canadian embassy to apply for a visa. It would take months for the application to be processed, they said. They would notify me of the outcome. "Where are you staying?" the clerk asked.

"I am not staying anywhere," I informed him. Suddenly, I realized the yawning gap in my escape plan, namely that my plan had never extended beyond getting out of Romania. My ultimate goal was to join my parents in Canada, but how, exactly, would I get from here to there?

Back on the street, I took stock of my circumstances. From my pocket I pulled a handful of leis, which were worthless here. In my briefcase I had a toothbrush and a change of underwear. Beyond that, I did not know one person in all of Greece and I did not speak the language. I stood on a bustling Athens street corner with my head spinning. At long last, I had escaped Romania and was now free, but free to do what?

I remembered that Katty had once waited for me here, imagining that I would flee Romania to her waiting arms to build a life together. What would it have been like if she had been here now to greet me? How warm her kisses would have been, how comforting the embrace of her Greek life.

It felt as though I had already hurtled through so many turns of fate in my young life, with so many opportunities, moments, and weighty decisions littering my past. Who could have foreseen, on that day when Father first took me to boarding school in Bucharest and admonished me to make him proud, that my life would have taken such a zigzag course? Now, I was a pauper alone in a strange country.

I walked the streets for many hours, and finally presented myself at the registration desk of a cheap hotel and asked to speak with the manager. I did not have any money for a room, I told him—communicating with him in French—but if he allowed me to make a telephone call to Canada, I would get the funds to pay him. He gave me a hard look. The city teemed with penniless immigrants. I'm sure he wondered, who was this upstart to expect credit? Thankfully, he agreed, and minutes later I heard the voice of my Aunt Elka answering the phone in Winnipeg.

She was surprised and overjoyed to hear my voice and to learn of my escape from Romania. My parents were not home, she said, but she would immediately wire me $100. "See you soon," I said. In my mind I pictured her telling my parents. Mother would erupt with tears of joy, and Father nod with deepest satisfaction.

I took up residence in the hotel, which was in the slum section of Athens. The Red Light District was just down the block. Many of the hotel residents were immigrants or displaced persons, exiles from their own countries on their way to new lives elsewhere in the world. Most dreamed of going to the West, primarily the United States or Canada. There was a strong sense that we were all in transition, in a limbo between lives we were leaving behind and new lives we had yet to discover.

These common circumstances created a bond among us. As was the case with many people in that part of the world, we all spoke several languages and could communicate reasonably well. We celebrated the New Year together, all of us crowded into the hotel's common kitchen, everyone cooking up a favorite dish. How excited we were to welcome in 1959, how rich it seemed with possibilities. I had become friends with a Turkish fellow in the hotel. We shared several bottles of wine that night, talking about our past lives and what we wanted for the future. My father was a wealthy cattle dealer living in Canada, I confided to him. Perhaps I would go into business with him. He was Jewish, my new-found friend explained, and his dream was to live in Israel.

* * *

My visa application received approval swiftly. Surprisingly, the Canadian ambassador was from Winnipeg and knew my uncle, who was a doctor there. The embassy had a file on me and knew much about my circumstances in Romania. So did the CIA. I had to undergo a debriefing with them, as apparently, did all immigrants arriving from Communist countries. It was a mere formality, since they already knew more about my family than I did. Some years later, when my friend Silviu would finally leave Romania, he would be detained for two years in Italy, undergoing repeated interviews with the CIA, before he too eventually landed in Canada.

Despite the approval of my application for immigration to Canada, I spent three months waiting for a visa. They were three very pleasant months. The contrast between Greece and Romania was so striking. Greece was what Romania used to be. Even among the poorest elements of society, I found vitality and hope.

I met a woman named Christina, a Greek from Romania who served as my tour guide, showing me the ancient ruins of the city, taking me home to share meals with her family. She was a secretary at the British embassy and claimed to have lost her virginity to the ambassador.

So many Greeks had lived in Romania. Many, like Christina, had been born and lived their whole lives there, while still maintaining Greek citizenship. When the Communists took over, these Greeks chose to leave. I met many of them in Athens.

The Greek owner of a restaurant named Bucharest visited me. He knew my father and had heard that I was in town. "How is your father? What is he doing?" he asked. In truth, I knew very little about how my father was or what he was doing. The content of our letters had always avoided anything of substance. But I knew he had taken a small fortune with him, and that the family was known to the ambassador. So, I assured the restaurant owner that my father was in Canada and doing very well.

One night, he closed his restaurant early and threw a party for me, inviting many Greeks who had once called Romania home, many who knew of my family. The celebration was warm and rowdy. We ate and drank to excess and danced far into the night. Maybe it was just a general level of goodwill that animated the group that night, but at least for me, it felt as though I had something very definite to celebrate—being out of Romania. That one fact alone made my spirits soar.

Towards the end of the evening, the restaurant owner laid a hand across my shoulder and said, "When you see your father, tell him what I did for you." Flattered by his attention, pleased that my father enjoyed such respect from this man, I assured him that I would. Before long, I had that opportunity. My visa came through, I took a flight to Canada, and after twelve years, had a tearful reunion with my parents in Winnipeg.

Father loaded my suitcase into the trunk of a shiny Pontiac automobile, and I remember thinking—what a luxurious car. Father is still a big shot, even in America. I could tell he was proud of the vehicle. However, I was taken aback by the tiny, one-bedroom apartment they lived in. It certainly did not fit with their old lifestyle.

It was near dinner time when I arrived, and my mother immediately busied herself in the kitchen, while Father sat me down in the living room, with a serious look upon his face. "Son," he said somberly, "we need to talk." I couldn't remember Father ever using quite that tone of voice before. "There has been a . . . a change in our circumstances. All of our wealth is gone." It was like Father to be so direct, but

I sat there blankly waiting for further explanation, unable or unwilling to process this information.

"I blundered in a business deal and lost everything."

"Everything?" I repeated that awful word, and he nodded solemnly. It seemed inconceivable that nearly half a million dollars could have vanished.

"I made a deal with a Canadian businessman. We bought a large farm and livestock. The U.S. market would soon open to Canadian beef, and we would be in a position to make a killing." He explained that shortly thereafter he had landed in the hospital for a prostate operation. When he came out a week later, everything was gone.

"'I had to sell out,' my partner told me. 'Your share has been lost,'" he said. Father was furious. He knew he was being swindled. He had never before encountered someone who did not honor their word. The deal had been struck Romanian-style with only a handshake. Nothing was on paper. Father complained to local authorities, and they called him foolish for not getting the agreement in writing.

It seemed odd to consider that here was a man who had traded with the Nazis to save my friend from Treblinka, who had dealt with the occupying Russian army, and sold cattle to the Communist government. Ten thousand handshakes striking deals with ten thousand desperately poor, uneducated peasants, and not once had he encountered a person who dishonored their word. How could you anticipate such perfidy? What did a man have without honor?

I was too angry, too confused, too gripped by Father's emotional story to think straight. What kind of country was this? Obviously one more predatory than Romania. What would we have to do, how would we have to change, to survive here? What did the future now hold for any of us?

After he had been swindled, he took a job with a railroad loading coal; later he became a junk dealer. Mother had gone to work as a seamstress. Money was tight, and Mother kept them on a very careful budget. He offered this so matter of factly. I knew he didn't want to be blamed or pitied, but I couldn't help thinking what a humiliation this was for a man who had been so successful and so widely known and respected in his home country.

"But now I have been going to the auctions again, watching the cattle market." He forced out a smile when he said that, as if to minimize the impact of the lost fortune, or to suggest it could be easily restored.

Even as he spoke, my mind brought back stories mother used to tell me as a child about Father's up and down business success, making fortunes, losing fortunes. It had all seemed so romantic back then, the stuff of legend. However, sitting face to face with the reality of it didn't seem nearly as glamorous as Mother's stories.

A thousand thoughts assailed me as I lay on the living room sofa that night. Anger bubbled near the surface. I wanted to do something to help my father, to correct this injustice. I wanted to confront that businessman, have him arrested, beat him up. Whatever it took.

I also felt guilt. All those years my parents had been sending me 100 dollars monthly, it had been coming, not from their boundless resources, but from their meager earnings. They must have been counting their pennies to afford it and doing without things just to help me get by. They had never said anything, or I wouldn't have taken the money. I couldn't help but imagine how well the scenario would have played with the communist censor who would have read the letters from overseas if my parents had written to tell me the truth. To hear a tale of an unscrupulous capitalist businessman, would have warmed the censor's heart.

This turn of events changed everything. I fretted and planned a good deal that sleepless night. Out the window went my dream of re-gaining the comfortable life my family once enjoyed in Romania. I resolved that I would not be a burden on my parents. The first order of business would be to find employment and get an income.

But how would I do that? Where were the jobs? How did one get them? I wanted to act quickly, but the most basic things seemed like insurmountable obstacles? What papers would I need? How could I find work if I did not speak English? Certainly Canadian factories did not need economic planners.

I could not bring myself to speak to my parents about this. The following day I visited my aunt and had her write a letter in good English, explaining that although I did not speak the language, I wanted a job and was a hard worker. I took this letter around to several factories before finally visiting the Coca Cola plant. The manager read the letter, looked me over and shook his head, then called the fore-man and told him to find work for me. Within 24 hours of arriving in Canada, I had a job.

I had one bit of unfinished business before I settled completely into the routine of a new job. I learned that although the businessman who had cheated my father was no longer in town, his son practiced dentistry in Winnipeg. I visited his office to yell at him about what a dishonorable bastard his father was, and getting no satisfaction, I trashed his office, upsetting, throwing, and breaking things. It was a childish display, but I felt so frustrated and helpless over what had happened that I needed an outlet for my rage.

My father and uncle were furious. They gave me an angry lecture on the legal system. "Mark, you could get away with things like that in Romania, but you're not in Romania any more. Here, that kind of behavior is a crime. You could get sued or land in jail." I had just received Lesson #1 in immigrant adjustment.

There was so much to admire about life in Canada, but I didn't particularly like this first lesson. Namely, that someone could swindle you out of your life savings and you were helpless to do anything about it, not even vent your anger.

* * *

I worked at Coca Cola for sixteen months. If I close my eyes, I can still see the cases of glass bottles rolling by. One of my jobs was to clean and wash the bottles. Sweep floors, stack cases, load trucks— much of the hard and me-nial work fell to me. I did not mind. I was so intent on making money that I volunteered for all the overtime I could get. Some days began at 5 a.m. and went to 12:30 a.m. For the first several months it was almost more than my body could take. I would drag myself home and fall asleep in the bathtub while soaking my aching muscles in hot water, catching a few precious hours of sleep until the alarm rang and the routine began all over again.

I had learned enough words in English by then to follow the few basic commands of my co-workers. "Go," "Sweep," "Over there." Most of the men were friendly. Many of them were second generation European immigrants whose families had fled earlier spasms of war, revolution, or poverty. I tended to associate them with their heritage and remember them now as "The German" or "The Russian."

It was the Russian who gave me an especially hard time. To him I was an ignorant foreigner who could not even speak the language, a servant to do his bidding. Never allowing me a moment's rest, even when everyone else paused for a break, he would constantly order me around, find some remote corner of the factory that wasn't as clean as he liked. I took this abuse for some time before finally losing my patience. One day while everyone was sitting down to a coffee break, and he ordered me to continue working, I dumped a bucket of water on his head. It had the desired effect. From that moment on, he left me alone.

Obviously, I was going to have trouble learning Lesson #1.

The incident in the dentist's office and the run-in with The Russian illustrate a volatile side of my personality. It was more than just a cultural difference. My temper has a low flash point. My actions, and my words, occasionally spring forth on impulse. Sometimes, as with The Russian, such action seems justified; other times I wish I could take back some deed or word that has served no useful purpose other than to display my irritation. Regardless, the trait has become a fixture of my personality.

I lived a spartan existence while working at Coca Cola, surviving on $8 a week. As soon as possible I took my own apartment. Without credit or references, I was unable to rent in a decent neighborhood. Sixty dollars a month—more than I would have paid in a good neighborhood—got me an apartment in the slums. Father was after me to get a better apartment; he would arrange it, loan me money. He didn't understand that I didn't want his help. I was a man now, not the university student he had left behind in Romania.

Most of my money went into savings. I would need it when I enrolled at the university. The men at the plant laughed at my plans to attend the university, especially since I could barely speak English. But, in my own mind, no doubt existed.

There have been periods in my life when I have felt myself in a holding pattern and have been without long-term goals. During these times, I have indulged in the pursuit of more immediate pleasures, and have thoroughly enjoyed myself. What lingers in my memory from those periods are the people. I feel a remarkably strong connection to old friends and lovers who have traveled along with me through a part of my life.

But there have also been periods when all of my energies have concentrated on a single task, anything from doing well in boarding school to surviving at Pereprava. Immediate pleasures took a back seat during these periods. A priority shift occurs. A goal is in sight, and other things get sacrificed. What I tend to remember from these periods is the work and hardship. They became a reward in themselves, taking me closer to my goal. The more I pushed my body towards exhaustion by working overtime at Coca Cola, the more I deprived myself to save money, the closer I approached my goal of enrolling at the university.

As for the more carefree days of the past. I dreamed about them a great deal, reliving the times I spent with Katty or Puica, the adventures of childhood, the revelry of my university years. I did not brood upon them; instead, they became a tool of survival, a pleasant diversion to distract me from the lack of pleasure in my life.

I corresponded with Puica, who still lived in Bucharest. A strong affection still existed between us, not romance so much as an enduring friendship of two who had been through so much together. She was desperate to give her life new direction, to free herself of the repressiveness of life in Communist Romania. Of course, we could not talk about these things in letters. I could not tell her of the exhilaration of freedom, and she could not lament her disenchantment with her life. But we read these things between the lines.

Eventually, Puica found a way out of Romania. With my help, she entered Canada and settled in Winnipeg. I was glad to have an old friend in this new land. Now and then, our old emotions rose up like the tide. Puica wanted us to get back together again. It seemed that fate was pushing us in that direction. But I resisted, remembering all the times we had tried in the past, all the times we had felt this way before and been unable to make it work. So, we remained good friends. She changed her medical specialty from general practice to psychiatry, and I watched from a distance over the next few years as she achieved much success and took up residence in Montreal.

* * *

Meanwhile, my father had been making small cattle trades. He had begun to develop a network of farmers who came to know and trust him. He would drive around to their farms, buy cattle, have them trucked to market, and make some money. It wasn't much of a livelihood, and money was still very tight for my parents, but it was very satisfying for him to again be working in the trade that he knew and enjoyed. When I went to their apartment for dinner, talk of cattle, farmers, and auctions animated his conversation, the way it had done back in Braila, when everything was right with the world.

After dinner, we would settle down to watch TV. I had never seen a television until I arrived in Canada. My father loved to watch professional wrestling. "It's fake," I said, but that didn't matter to him. The arm-twisting, head-banging action fascinated him.

Eventually I bought a TV for my own apartment, and it became my window on this new culture. I had earlier enrolled in a course to learn English, but found it too mindlessly slow and ineffective. They seemed to think that not only was every immigrant ignorant of the language but unintelligent as well. So, I worked at teaching myself. When I was not working, my TV stayed on 24 hours a day. When I was not glued to the screen, sounding out the words spoken by actors and newscasters, the set played as background noise. The contents of the programs meant nothing to me; I did not understand the things they referred to. But I wanted to hear the words, to have the rhythms of the language echoing in my head.

Anyone who has ever struggled to learn English as a second language, knows how frustrating it can be. I knew French and German well. I had gained a passable command of Russian in only six months. But English is such a mongrel collection of foreign words, a language with more exceptions than rules for spelling and grammar. It challenged me for many years. It still challenges me.

* * *

Occasionally, Father's driving excursions took him past my apartment on a weekend, and he would stop in for a visit. It's hard to explain the changes that had come over Father since leaving Romania. He was in his 60s now, but he was also a different person from the man I had put on an airplane in Bucharest in 1948. His experiences in Canada had taken something out of him. Or maybe it was a combination of all his experiences since losing his property to the Communists. Different governments, different countries, different business climates, cut off from his network of friends and associates, constrained by the limitations of a new language—he did not exude the same boundless confidence. Although life had taught him a few more lessons, no longer did he spout them as cryptic maxims for his son.

"Mark, I find myself in a tight spot," he said one Saturday at my apartment. "My car had repairs last month, but it needs more work, $75 they tell me. You know how your mother is about pinching pennies. I'd rather not tell her about this if I can take care of it myself. You understand."

I understood perfectly, but that did not lessen the impact of that moment. The car represented a great deal to my father. It was a symbol of his independence, and of course a necessary tool for cattle trading. But he could not bring himself to tell Mother that they had to tap their meager resources so that he could keep it on the road. And so, he did something that went very much against his grain, something that he had never done before, he asked to borrow money from me.

I immediately wrote out a check. The whole transaction came off very matter-of-factly. And yet, it was humiliating for Father and painfully embarrassing for me. Moments like that burn themselves into memory with their unspoken significance. If Father was no longer spouting his maxims of life, he was now demonstrating them. And the message was clear: *never* permit yourself to be this financially vulnerable.

*   *   *

I knew that my university degree, the licentiate, would not be sufficient to build a career in the West. I arranged for an interview with the chairman of the Sociology / Anthropology Department at the University of Manitoba. My English was still so poor that I had to take along a friend to translate. "How do you expect to study here if you don't even know the language?" the chairman asked.

"Tell him, I'll know English by Christmas," I said to the translator. "If I don't he can throw me out."

The Chairman looked amused. "I want to see this miracle," he said, and accepted me into the program.

A graduate fellowship eased my economic crunch. In fact, I had enough money to buy a car. Father made a show of selecting for me the best used car on the lot. In actuality, he knew as much about the mechanical operation of cars as I did—next to nothing—and the car turned out to be a lemon. Still, being a graduate student with my own car, I was on top of the world.

Opportunity was presenting itself, doors were opening, the possibility of a bright future was rising out of the confusion, but everything depended on my ability to master the English language. Lectures were gibberish to me, textbooks yielded their wisdom only after laborious word-by-word translation. Could I live up to the boast I had made to the chairman? And if I didn't, would I be sentenced to a life of washing Coca Cola bottles?

In memory, it seems that mastering English became my sole obsession during the fall of 1961. The task acquired a symbolic value. It is an issue familiar to every immigrant down through history. Language is the key to integration into the new country. Those who speak fluently can learn, communicate their needs, use the system. Those who cannot speak the language, are at a greater risk of being exploited or ignored.

Romanian was still spoken in my parents's home. Being forced to communicate on the job—and watching TV—had given Father a basic grasp of English, but Mother lacked the motivation to learn a new language. The need was too small or the effort too large. She seemed content to live in the narrower confines of the immigrant world. There were enough people in her life who spoke one of the languages of Europe that she understood.

Mother, too, had changed in the intervening years. No longer was she the proud woman who had presided over the large household in Braila, passing along the colorful heritage of the family. That house had disappeared and the heritage lost some of its color. Mother's pride had slipped beneath the surface and transformed to profound disappointment. But this transformation was masked by her stoicism.

My parents had some friends but very few of them were Romanians. Although other Romanians lived in Winnipeg, we had little contact with them. "They might be Iron

Guard or Nazis," Father warned. He wanted nothing to do with them, and of course nothing to do with the current government of Communists.

It was this period in the life of my family that ignited in me an interest in the immigrant experience. Unlike some immigrant groups, we had no lingering attachments to the homeland. We had no family still living there. We had no religious affiliations. We had brought no grand traditions or celebrations from the Old World. About all that survived was a wistful nostalgia for the way of life we had enjoyed before the war. We existed in a limbo between complete estrangement from our homeland and integration into our new country. It was an unsettling place to be. A place without power or security.

My own struggle with the language was a considerable hurdle, but slowly meaning began to emerge through the words. Some of the writers I studied, such as Durkheim and Weber I had read before. But even after I began to understand my texts, I still could not articulate my thoughts in English.

After one test, the professor called me into his office and said that there was a problem with my test. He suspected me of cheating, but was reluctant to come right out and say it. Instead he asked me to retake the test. When he had corrected that second test, he called me in again.

"Mark, what is going on here? I asked you to retake the test because your answers the first time were almost word for word from the textbook. I thought you had copied. But this second test is exactly the same."

"A very easy explanation," I said. "I memorized the words. All 2,500 pages of text, I could write down as it appears in the textbooks," I explained. "I understand them, but to explain, or even rephrase, them in English is impossible for me." I think he was amused by my approach and sympathetic to my predicament. "I will teach you English," he said. From then on he took special pains to work with me and give me oral exams.

In my second semester, I was given a teaching fellowship, and took my first abortive step into the classroom.

Not surprisingly, the students could not understand the mangled English of my lectures. The sociology department thought it better for me to abandon that effort and pursue a research project.

I was assigned as a research associate on an interesting study of immigrant populations in northern Manitoba. The study would examine the value systems of three immigrant groups—Icelanders, Ukrainians, and Germans—that had settled in the rugged area between Lake Manitoba and Lake Winnipeg (the Inter-Lake Region) between 1875 and World War I.

I was delighted. I longed to do field research. In addition, here was a project where my language skills would be an asset rather than a hindrance, since I spoke both German and Russian.

I still recall the neat, well-organized farms of the Germans. The barn was often in better condition than the house, all the income going to advancing the farming business. The Ukrainians paid less attention to the maintenance of their farms than they did to the maintenance of their souls. Religious icons and pictures of Christ hung in all their homes; their farms always looked a bit run down. When I visited, the man of the house would sit down with me for the interview, while the wife hovered in the background. If there was a son over 15 years of age, he too might participate.

These immigrants had come to a new country, created new communities when farming was a way of life, when individuals were bound by ethnic origin and by mutual dependence. But now the modern world was reshaping their lives and beliefs. With the advent of farm machinery, farming was becoming less a way of life, than a way to make a living. From every side forces were slowly integrating them into Canadian culture, eroding their traditional values.

I often saw parallels to my own family. Some comment or observation would remind me of the Bessarabian village of Arciz where my parents grew up. Bessarabia had possessed its own distinct German colonies. The German farms were always flourishing; they owned the best horses. Their Russian neighbors were less adept at running successful farms, perhaps because they devoted too much of their time to drinking. Ironically, in light of later developments, it was the German farmers who were the friends and protectors of local Jews, and the Russians who terrorized them with pogroms.

Although my parents had not moved to a new country, they had chosen to break with their ancestral roots in Arciz by moving to Braila. Father had wanted a better life for himself and his children, just as these Manitoba farmers did. In many ways I felt close to these Canadian immigrants that I was studying, as though we sprang from the same European tradition and faced similar struggles adapting to life in a new home.

My work with those farmers seemed to put me in touch with the very essence of the immigrant experience, the raw energy of hope and determination that had built the greatness of Canada and the U.S. The lives of these transplanted peasants represented the tens of millions of people who had come to the New World seeking a second chance in life.

While doing my field work that fall, I stayed at a small cabin by a beautiful lake. I had met a German woman back in Winnipeg. On weekends, she drove up to be with me. She was trapped in a loveless marriage and had arranged to enjoy her time with me with the full knowledge of her husband.

We had our own little corner of the world, a romantic wilderness. In the mornings, when chill was in the air and mist shrouded the lake, I would stand outside the cabin and survey the endless expanse of water and woodlands and imagine how it must have felt to come here seventy years before as a pioneer.

For those who had come from repressive homelands, for those undaunted by the amount of work their dreams represented, this must have been an earthly paradise. Such moments always draw from me the fantasy of owning a large estate, being master over a farming operation. Becoming a gentleman farmer has never been an actual goal, but more an elemental part of my psyche. As if buried beneath my own happy experiences on the farm, there exists the collective consciousness of my peasant ancestors, calling me to such endeavors.

I rediscovered something about myself during that research—my love of intellectual challenge. Circumstances had certainly put my life on a roller coaster ride over the past 15 years. But being stimulated by this research recalled my best experiences at boarding school and the university and gave me a feeling of confidence that my life was back on track.

It was as though I had taken a detour early in my education at the University of Bucharest—a long detour of the gulag, aimless years of unemployment and black marketeering, a stint as a factory planner, a Coca Cola bottle washer—and only now had I returned to the right course.

In a way, it suggested a parallel between my life and my father's up and down business success. Seeing parallels between my parents and myself is a habit I have indulged in frequently as the years have gone by. I'm willing to acknowledge them as the source of all my best traits and accept that the bad ones I have cultivated on my own.

At that point in my life, however, it was Father's quality of persistence that struck a chord in me. His unrelenting work, optimism, and ambition have always inspired me. I felt the motive force of his character urging me on as I launched my academic career. My mother's pride and stubbornness added to the strength I found in my parents as role models.

My father, meanwhile, was enjoying more success at cattle dealing. He was more active and happy, making contacts with more farmers around Winnipeg. Slowly, an increasing network of farmers were beginning to trust and depend on him to buy their cattle.

It was an easy step to imagine that the Iutcovich fortunes were on the rise. I was preparing for an academic career, and Father rebuilding his traditional business. Father was so pleased with his success one day that he called my mother from the cattle market. "I had a very good day," he reported with enthusiasm. I made $600. We will celebrate when I get home."

Except that he did not get home. One hour passed, then two. Mother began to worry. Then a call from the hospital informed her that Father had suffered a heart attack. I was summoned, and together we watched him cling desperately to life for three days before dying.

The agonizing bedside death watch tore out my mother's heart. She had always deeply loved Father, but the years of exile had brought them even closer together. In Braila they had each had their own distractions, each gone their own way. But being immigrants in a strange land had forced them to be more dependent upon each other. And the financial hardship of surviving their lost fortune provided the bond of additional shared misfortune.

Mother never recovered from the loss of Father. She dragged herself through each day in the grip of severe depression. She could not bear to live alone and so accepted my Aunt Elka's invitation to live with her. That was not to her liking, but what could she do? She did not want to be a burden on me. Besides, what did it matter, really? She felt that her life was over. Elka, being a physician, could prescribe the sleeping pills that provided the only way for her to escape the torment of sleeplessness, the only solace she could find.

I visited her often and tried to be cheerful and find a topic of conversation that would spark her interest. I was wrapping up my research with the Ukrainian and German farmers. Sometimes I would tell her about the farmers, and it would trigger for us a vivid memory of my childhood when Leon, Misha, and I huddled around Mother to hear her stories of the family, about the good times and the hard times she and Father had endured.

10
A Land of Immigrants

My old Dodge pulled into the dirt drive of the small house belonging to Maniu Todescu. A large dog ran up to my car and announced my arrival with insistent barking. My Research Methods class had made no mention of how to handle angry dogs.

I had arranged this interview through another Romanian farmer living in the area. I had phoned the previous day to let Todescu know that I was coming. I waited in the car until a face appeared at the door to call off the dog, then I gathered my notebooks, stepped out, and greeted him in Romanian.

I was in the Shell Valley of northern Manitoba conducting field research for my Master's thesis. This region had been dense forest when Romanian immigrants settled here around the turn of the century, but they had cleared the land, prospered, and been largely assimilated into Canadian society. I wanted to study that process of acculturation. How did immigrants adjust to life in a new country? How much of a role did their past culture play in their lives, and how was it blended with the new culture? Through what processes did they adapt?

My study would compare the Romanian experience with that of the Hutterites, a religious sect that emigrated to this area at about the same time as the Romanians but chose to live in isolated communities, under strict religious authority.

Obviously, being an immigrant in a new country was familiar territory to me. The year was 1962, and I had called

Canada home for almost three years. One of the disadvantages of being a sociologist is a heightened awareness of the forces acting upon yourself. Sometimes you feel less a participant in life than an observer, always once removed from your own experiences. This "marginalism" was doubly true for me, being an outside observer as both a sociologist and a new immigrant.

Ever since entering graduate school in Canada, I had noted with increasing fascination my own adjustment to life in my new country. When I had to pick a subject for my graduate research, it seemed only natural to select an area to which I felt so personally connected. Studying these immigrant families was revealing something about my own future as well, a future that sometimes filled me with anxiety. What new lessons had yet to be learned in this new land?

One curious difference between myself and most immigrant groups was that they attempted to preserve their values and attachments to the Old World, whereas I was intent on fitting into my new home as quickly and fully as possible. About the only thing I wanted desperately to preserve from Romania was my mother.

Just prior to beginning my research, I had been spending much time with her. As often as possible I stopped by my aunt's house. "She's still having trouble sleeping," Aunt Elka would whisper, then shake her head to indicate her grave concern over how mother was dealing with Father's death. I too felt my father's loss very deeply. Physically or emotionally my parents had always been at the center of my universe. Father's death, six months earlier, had blasted a hole in my life. But at least I had other things in my life to distract me and to give me hope.

Mother, on the other hand, had never lifted out of her despondency. I kept looking for signs of the emotional healing to begin, but never saw them. Life simply did not make sense for her without my father. Even when I could light a spark of interest in some conversation, it seemed more a gesture for my benefit.

When I told her about the Romanian peasants I would be studying, she listened with curiosity. The circumstances of their immigration interested her. The miserable condition of the peasant in Romania and the disruption of World War I drew a knowing response. She associated it with the hardships of being an immigrant herself and the difficult lessons it taught—the loss of their fortune, her working as a seamstress, and her feelings of isolation. She was not pleased that I was living in northern Manitoba for an extended period during the study. But disappointment seemed only to disperse into the vastness of her depression.

One morning that spring I arrived at my Aunt's house late in the morning, and my mother was still not up. A dark feeling of foreboding passed over me, and I raced up to her room. She lay unconscious in bed. I put up the alarm and had her rushed to the hospital. She had been saving her sleeping pills and then had taken them all at once.

When I got the dreaded phone call from a doctor at the hospital, informing me that Mother had died, I murmured, "What do I do now?" I suppose he thought my question referred to the complications of funeral arrangements. He could not have been more wrong. The question stabbed to the existential core of my being. What did life mean for me now that both my parents were gone? Now that I was alone in this foreign land.

At the time I was writing my final examination and working on my thesis. When the department chairman learned of my mother's death, he suggested that I take time off to deal with the tragedy. I didn't want time off, I told him, work was the only way I had of dealing with the tragedy. In fact, I needed to be twice as busy, twice as distracted, to keep from coming apart.

My uncle suggested that I use the $5,000 inheritance I received to help pay for my education, since I intended to go on for my Ph.D. For much of my life, I had relied on my parents, but taking this final offering did not seem right. I spent the entire amount, every cent, for a marble tombstone. Memories would always keep them alive for me, but memories seemed insufficient for so great a loss. I wanted a grander and more permanent monument in stone to the lives of Joseph and Mathilda Iutcovich.

* * *

Todescu filled his kitchen table with bread, cheese, jam and sausage, then sat down to await my questioning. He was in his seventies and had come to Canada in 1909. He had been born a peasant in Transylvania in 1889, when that Romanian province was under the control of the Austro-Hungarian Empire. It had been a hard life. Like most peasants, his family had owned no land, but worked for bare subsistence wages for a large landowner. The privileges in society went to the Hungarian and German majorities. His family had not even spoken the Magyar language of their government.

Todescu's family emigrated to the Kingdom of Romania in the 1890s. But economic conditions were little better there. That's when the Canadian government began advertising in Romania for immigrants. "I saw a poster," Todescu told me, "Come to Canada, it said, and we will give you land." My interview was stirring Todescu's memories of 60 years ago. "I came alone, a young man out to make his fortune. There were already other Romanian families in this area. We were a very close community." He knew English well, but for my benefit spoke in Romanian, actually an odd hybrid language of Romanian peppered with English.

It was late in the 19th century that the Canadian government had gone to eastern Europe to find "sheepskin" peasants. The term was an allusion to the sheepskin coats often worn by peasants in parts of Europe. Canada was intent on opening its prairie wilderness to agriculture and was looking for people who would not shirk from the isolation of the pioneering life nor the backbreaking toil of clearing dense forests. Canadians were not standing in line to volunteer for that dirty work.

But the promise of free land brought a wave of new immigrants enthusiastic about taking on the challenge, including Manitoba's Romanians.

"When I first arrived, I was always thinking to go back to Romania." Todescu resumed his story. "'One thousand dollars and the fare' was what we said. Stay in Canada just long enough to save $1,000 and the boat fare to return home. Then we would buy land and live a good life. But your plans do not always turn out." He shrugged. "Sometimes events ambush you. Things were not so good back home, then came the war. Now I have been here more than fifty years." He paused for a moment of reflection. "Romania? What can I say? I am a Canadian now."

My whole summer was devoted to gathering information about this community of Romanians and their Hutterite neighbors. I began by making repeated visits, establishing contacts, friendships, before asking the sort of probing questions I needed to learn about their experiences. I talked to some of the original settlers, their children, and, at least with some Romanians, their Canadian wives. I was learning valuable lessons about conducting field work, how best to win the trust of a group and get them to share their stories.

The Hutterites required a different approach. They lived communally on large farming estates. Couples / families lived in rooms within large houses, all presided over by strict religious leaders that guarded their adherence to the faith. How would a sociologist gain the confidence of such a closed community? I recalled a lesson from my father.

He had been buying cattle from a Hutterite community. To win the cooperation of its religious leader, he had given him a gift of whiskey. The Hutterites are very much like the Amish, wearing a similar plain clothing, eschewing many modern conveniences. Alcohol is strictly forbidden. But, following Father's lead, I took a bottle of fine Canadian whiskey along for my first visit to the leader. Anything for science, I reasoned, even corrupting the Holy. It had the desired effect. Pleased with my token of friendship, he granted my request to speak with his flock about their experiences adjusting to life in the New World. Every future visit I made to the commune, I took along another bottle to assure continued cooperation.

A strong vein of cynicism has grown in my personality over the years, and nothing has done more to encourage its growth than my contact with any group of "True Believers," those who believe that their ideology or faith has shown them the one and only true path for getting through life. On the whole, I have found them the most hypocritical, least compassionate, and sometimes, the most evil creatures on the face of the earth.

The Hutterite move from Europe to Canada was more a change of geography than a transplant to a new culture. All the force of the Hutterite community was directed at maintaining a central core of beliefs and practices *separate* from the surrounding society. The men I spoke with wore beards; their clothes and surroundings lacked any pretense of design or comfort. They spoke quite openly about their experiences and beliefs, and the operation of the commune.

The church community controlled every aspect of life: the economic system, the school, social structure, customs, etc. They considered themselves the chosen people of God ("God's Little Flock") and for that reason chose to remain isolated. Contact with the larger community for them meant the contamination and the corruption of their pure Christian principles. Women and children always huddled in the background. I'd glimpse them peeking around doorways and peering from windows at this stranger in their midst. As though I was as alien as a visitor from space.

But the modern age was intruding. More roads extended into the area, and electricity, radio, and telephone brought the surrounding culture even closer. Hutterite leaders bowed to the inevitable in certain areas, readjusting their interpretation of what was permissible to include such modern conveniences as electricity or central heating. They could accept change but sought to control the type and speed of that change. It was a policy that was meeting with only partial success. Since each successive generation showed a greater tolerance of change, and the change was becoming increasingly insistent, it seemed that the colony and its unique culture was heading for eventual dissolution.

Living in Manitoba that summer, I felt unattached to most everything but my work. As with my earlier study of immigrants in the inter-lake region, I once again identified with the people I studied. The connection was even stronger this time. The values of the Romanian peasants were the values I had been raised with: strong family orientation, strong work ethic, the importance of family prestige, a tradition of hospitality and generosity. The farm environment of the Hutterites recalled the idyllic years I had spent on our family farm in Braila.

I sometimes imagine that if some inquiring graduate student would study the process of my integration into my new culture, he or she would find that it was swift but never complete. Those "peasant" values still guide my behavior, and comparisons between my old homeland and my new haunt me nearly every day.

And yet in other ways I felt worlds apart from these immigrants. Both the Hutterites and Romanians were members of an ethnic group, a group that supported and sustained them, and one that slowed, or actively resisted, their integration into Canadian society. I had no such group. Unlike them, I had no lingering attachment to the Old World or to values of yesteryear. I sought a rapid integration into my new country.

As for the strong religious faith that sustained both groups, I had none. Once in my youth, I stood on the grave of my brother Misa and screamed, "There is no god!" That sentimental launch into atheism was hardened in later years by a logical rejection of religion. Tragedy and logical analysis had brought my mother to the same viewpoint.

*   *   *

I arrived in Toronto in 1963, a doctoral candidate in sociology at the University of Toronto. Manitoba felt like a closed chapter of my life, a transitional period between my old life filled with Romania and my parents, and a new life on my own in North America.

But part of my old life found me in Toronto. Christina, the Greek woman I had met in Athens, arrived in the city. We renewed our relationship. Christina was a fascinating blend of Old World and New. Old values of relationships and home existed along with an independent spirit. Her work experience and her ability to speak English like a native had gotten her a position with the Red Cross.

These were years of stability as I worked my way through the doctoral program, quiet years of course work and Christina's wonderful cooking. Christina usually served as editor for my research papers, putting my stumbling English into more polished form. An image of my future began to take shape. A Ph.D. in sociology from the University of Toronto, an academic discipline that was just establishing itself in America, would lead to a choice academic appointment. I would enjoy a good life of comfortable respectability, continue my research, and make a mark for myself in the discipline.

Meanwhile, during this period, I heard again from the Hutterites I had studied earlier. They hired me as a consultant to advise on a problem. I drove back to northern Ontario to meet with them, a bottle of whiskey tucked into my suitcase. The problem was that they had too many women, the elders explained to me very somberly in one of the spare rooms of the commune. And too few men. I remembered all the times I had visited communal homes and how the women always lurked behind corners, as if overflowing available space.

More critical still, they explained, was that some of their flock had reinterpreted a biblical passage to permit polygyny and had taken several wives. This was more than a practical problem of too few young men, but struck at the foundation of their faith. What would I advise?

It seemed that even the holy believed in sex. Of course, religion and sexuality have often been in opposition. The challenge for the faithful is to find some "acceptable" way to accommodate the sexual needs of their flock.

I was flattered to be consulted on so grave a matter. But the advice I finally gave, after studying the problem, was a simple and practical solution that did not touch upon biblical interpretation or matters of faith. Correct the unequal distribution of the sexes by exchanging men and women with other Hutterite communities, such as those in Manitoba. They took my advice. Women had mates; the faith was preserved.

Concerns about immigrant/ethnic groups continued to be the focus of my research. The Sociology Department undertook a research project sponsored by the Royal Commission on Bi-lingualism and Bi-culturalism. We would study the relationship between the French and English speaking peoples in northern Ontario and Quebec. Was there conflict or cooperation? To what extent were the French Canadians assimilating into the majority English Canadian culture? What was the social distance between the two groups? This was as critical a social and political issue then as it is now, given that it defined the nature of Canada and had significant political implications.

I was selected to head up the Ontario part of the project. The department chair—I'll call him Dr. Hilliard—drove me to Northern Ontario. Our study in this province would focus on a paper mill town that we would refer to as Milltown. Dr. Hilliard wanted to familiarize me with the community. Here was the French neighborhood, he said as he drove me around, and here was the mill. Most of the executives of the paper mill were English, who lived over here. And there was the town hall and there were the churches, a protestant church for the majority of the English-speaking population, and two Catholic churches. The French-speaking population worshipped at Notre Dame and the English-speaking Catholics at St. Patrick's. Fortunate that God was polyglot, I thought, or these Catholics would have been forced to worship in one church.

As he drove around pointing out the familiar landmarks, he also began to explain about the character of the town: the creation of the mill, the use of both English- and French- speaking workers, how the common goal of the mill had forced cooperation between these two diverse groups.

In fact, he went beyond background information and explained the nature of the relationship between the two groups that lived there. Harmony reigns, there is considerable mingling of the two groups, and eventually the French will be absorbed into the majority English culture. That was his assessment.

It bothered me that he already had a firm opinion on the very subject we were about to study. Proper objectivity is hardly served by such preconceived notions. But I didn't say anything. I would conduct the study and see if my findings supported his opinions.

To conduct my research, it was necessary to go undercover. I would pass myself off as an historian sent to study the town. People are often made self-conscious by, or are outright resistant to being studied by a sociologist. Whereas, an historian is just "recording facts," and people are often eager to get their story on the record.

So, I took an apartment in town, met with some of the prominent citizens, began to hang out at the cafe, which was something of a social hub of the community, and generally tried to become part of the town. Since my French was as good as my English, I could socialize with both populations and gradually began to fit in and make friends.

What I hadn't counted on was the brutal winter of northern Ontario. That took more adjustment than blending in socially. Temperatures dropped as low as -50 degrees. On one such day, I made the mistake of walking across the street without putting on my hat with fur-lined ear flaps. When I entered the cafe on the other side, my ears were big as cauliflowers, nearly frozen by their brief exposure. On another occasion, I foolishly decided to trek on snowshoes the few miles to the old site of the mill. I made it there all right, but struggled mightily to get back.

"You thought you had been cold at Pereprava," I said to myself, "but this is worse." The numbing cold sapped my energy, the wind and the effort of walking in the deepening snow challenged my strength. Uncertain of my direction, I felt a mounting panic. There were no buildings to duck into, only the vastness of empty tundra stretching around the town. I could easily have died on that occasion, one small sacrifice to the advance of sociology, but I finally made it back, a good deal wiser about northern winters.

The picture that began to emerge from the research was not all that surprising, given the long-standing antagonism between the French- and English-speaking populations of Canada. The conflicts existing between these two populations elsewhere in Canada existed here as well. Though industrialization brought them together, each population regarded the other as "strangers," culturally and linguistically different.

The English thought of themselves as the progressive force in the community whose mission it was to impose their culture on their French neighbors. The French considered their English neighbors as arrogant. The French had great pride in their own culture and were sensitive to any thought of assimilation into English culture.

Reality seemed to refute Dr. Hilliard's assumption that the joint economic mission of working in the mill would foster cooperation and assimilation. In fact, it had no special influence on the interaction of the two groups. Their social organization had little to do with economics. The French middle class, for instance, shared much less with the English middle class than it did with the rest of the French-speaking population, regardless of class. Nor did religion draw the two groups together. French Catholics socialized with their French-speaking neighbors, not with English speaking fellow Catholics. French-speaking Catholics worshipped at Notre Dame, and English-speaking Catholics at St. Patrick's. Even when the two groups shared the powerful binding forces of economic interest or religion, they still maintained social distance.

I returned to Toronto to write my report, aware that the findings would challenge Dr. Hilliard's assumptions, perhaps even the results that the government anticipated. That fact made me even more motivated to present a careful and persuasive account of my findings. I locked myself in my apartment, along with all necessary reference books, statistical reports, interview transcripts, and research notes, and set to work.

What a mountain of material. I had to be certain that it was presented carefully and that my conclusions were beyond refute. I read and reread the material, absorbing all the data, becoming so thoroughly consumed by my task that I lost track of time.

Christina, who lived about one block away, would leave food outside my door, along with pots of strong coffee, as the days went by. I chugged away like one possessed. Occasionally, I fell asleep over a notebook, but woke again in a few hours and resumed work. As the hand-written pages accumulated, I left them outside the door for Christina, who had begun to type the manuscript.

Everything was emerging so clearly. The history of the mill, the long-standing attitudes of these two populations, the special circumstances of Milltown, the social theories of Max Weber, Emile Durkheim, and Georg Simmel. I could take something from the academic literature, Bogardus's Social Distance Scale, for instance, and see how accurately it predicted the creation of boundaries between groups in a population. Everything blended together to form obvious conclusions.

Never before or since have I experienced a period of intellectual production and creativity that so fully consumed me. Nothing else existed in the world but my mind wrestling with the evidence and the argument of this project. When I had written the final page, I felt an enormous rush of satisfaction and relief. Everything was there, every possible scrap of evidence documented, explained, and interpreted to justify my conclusions. I handed over the last pages to Christina, pushed books and notes off the bed, and collapsed into a profound sleep for two days.

I couldn't have anticipated the storm my report would cause or what its impact would be on my life. A few days after I submitted it, Dr. Hilliard called me to his office. He did not accept my conclusions. The findings in Quebec had been just the opposite, indicating the gradual assimilation of French culture. I had obviously made mistakes.

"Also, you used statistics," he grumbled. "Take them out." He was a proponent of the journalistic school of sociology rather than the scientific school, and could not tolerate even the very basic statistical computations I had included in the report.

He demanded that I rethink my report, then rewrite it with the proper conclusion. I couldn't believe such stupidity. Or duplicity. I can't remember all the names I called him, though I did say that in Romania I wouldn't have hired him as my chauffeur. Soon the volume of our argument echoed in the halls. It ended with me quitting the doctoral program, and storming out of the building.

"I promise you will never earn your doctorate and never be a sociologist!" These were the chairman's final, shouted words to me.

All right, Iutcovich, what do you do now? I asked myself the next day, when my emotions had settled back to normal. Was this another immigrant lesson to be learned or the same one repeating itself? Suddenly, I was cut off, my plans put on hold. I had completed all the course work for my Ph'D, but did not have the degree. I had burned my bridges at the University. Would I have to start over in a doctoral program at another university? Could I still have an academic career?

What had Maniu Todescu told me to explain why he never returned to Romania? "Plans do not always turn out. Sometimes events ambush you." That was a healthy attitude. Roll with life's punches; make the most of what fate hands you.

Fate had certainly thrown me my share of curves, forcing changes in plans, sometimes forcing an abandonment of plans. Certainly one needs to be flexible. Yet, it goes so strongly against my nature to accept what life gives me, to allow my course to be dictated by whatever wind should happen to blow. I feel most alive when I am struggling to achieve some goal, resisting odds rather than surrendering to them. And few things had emerged more clearly in my character than the fact that I could not bring myself to bow to unreasonable authority, even when it might be in my best interest to do so.

To survive for the moment, I applied for teaching positions. It was late in the academic year and job opportunities were slim. But Mount Saint Joseph College in Cincinnati called me for an interview. It was a small, prestigious, Catholic girl's college. The interview went well, and they wanted to hire me, except for one problem. I did not have a green card to live and work in the United States.

The college president was a nun named Sister Mary Grace, who had the very best of political connections. She contacted a U.S. senator and arranged for me to be granted a special immigration status by claiming that my hiring was necessary to the national interest. Imagine that, I thought, this wayward academic, Mark Iutcovich, necessary for the national interest of the United States.

11
Among the Saints

On the surface, Cincinnati was a sober, God-fearing town, and the students at Mount St. Joseph were among the best the city and the surrounding region had to offer. They came from affluent families, professional families, some "old money." They had good high school educations, espoused conservative Catholic ideas, were well versed in etiquette, and generally displayed what would in another age have been referred to as "good breeding." I enjoyed having them as students. They came to class in pleated skirts and cashmere sweaters, sat properly erect at their desks, intelligent, attentive, and eager to learn.

The order of nuns that ran Mount St. Joseph's had come into a great deal of money not too many years earlier when they sold off some valuable property. The money had financed campus-wide construction. Everything was new and luxurious. The best classrooms, dormitories, and offices gave the clear impression that this was an elite school.

Mount St. Joseph was not a finishing school, but it seemed to share some of those goals. It provided a good liberal arts education within a religious context. Courses on religion, daily Masses, the presence of novices in the classes and nuns on campus exercised a restraining hand on the students. Curfews and restrictions on social activities assured that the students would keep their attention properly focused on whatever the nuns deemed important.

These girls came from solid upper middle-class and upper-class homes, and they would be given the sort of careful education necessary to prepare them to grace their own middle- and upper-class homes. The school, their families, and the times themselves conspired to better prepare the girls to be attractive assets to their husbands than to prepare them for careers. In this respect, Mount St. Joseph was not unlike many other American institutions of higher education in 1965.

Into this bastion of American respectability and rectitude came the Romanian peasant, atheist, intellectual, Professor Mark Iutcovich, preaching the gospel of social awareness. Sociology was still something of a novelty at some American colleges. The Mount had no courses in sociology when I arrived. So I was kept busy creating new courses and learning the fine points of the classroom.

For girls on the Mount, sociology seemed to have the lure of things alien and controversial, of ideas that challenged the tenets of their well-defined world. Social issues were rapidly rising to the top of the American agenda in the mid-1960s. That summer civil rights riots had erupted in Watts and Detroit. In fact, Cincinnati had its own share of slums and lower classes that had remained very much removed from the lives of these girls. Opposition to the war in Vietnam was coalescing. Betty Friedan had recently published *The Feminine Mystique* to usher in the age of feminism. What a stimulating context for teaching sociology in the Heartland of America.

My courses became very popular, and I acquired a colorful reputation among the faculty, administration, and students. Here, in their midst, was a foreigner who had lived under Nazism and Communism, served time in the gulag, and questioned the set answers on social issues these students had been provided. I wanted to challenge them, shock them if necessary, to force them to think about and rethink their beliefs. Some day abortion will be legal, I told them. When? When the Pope gets pregnant. After their initial shock, we could discuss the issue more objectively, and they would be forced to defend with logic the views they held on such issues.

In class, we discussed the most prevalent social issues of the day, without being judgmental, leaving matters of faith and prejudice behind for a scientific explanation. It did my heart good to watch these girls struggle to accommodate new ideas, to think about and defend the views that had simply been accepted from their parents, to confront social issues that had always stayed once removed from their comfortable lives.

I also taught part-time at Xavier College, an all-male Catholic school in Cincinnati. As a part-timer, I was less of a fixture on campus there, but I did become good friends with some of the priests, especially Father Leahy. Sandy-haired, gregarious, and fun-loving, he served as Dean of the college and was a respected academic in his own right. Along with several other priest / professors, he would drop by my apartment for drinks and conversation.

* * *

I drove Route 74 south, crossing over the Ohio River into Kentucky, heading for a town called Covington. Heavy Friday night traffic lined the road out of Cincinnati. Several people had told me about this town. They spoke its name as though it were one of the seven deadly sins, a den of vice. The suggestion was that when the god-fearing people of Cincinnati wanted some sinful fun, they made a pilgrimage to Covington. I had to see for myself.

Gaudy signs invited you into bars. Neon flashed advertisements for strip tease shows. My first reaction was: what a curiously American place. How very different it looked from that Bucharest den of vice, the whorehouse enshrined in my youth, where the prostitute Maria educated me in sex. That was a quiet experience, a natural order of life. By contrast, Covington's selling of sex seemed lurid and artificial. It reminded me instead of another of my childhood experiences, the time I had an unpleasant run-in with some professional women on the island of Malta.

Father and I had traveled to Malta with a shipment of sheep he planned to sell. The year was 1937, and I was a curious eight-year-old, delighted to accompany Father on one of his business trips.

A committee of Maltese merchants—perhaps resenting Father's intrusion into their market—had circulated a rumor that the sheep we were selling had been suckled on pigs' milk. It sounds silly to say it, but the rumor seriously threatened our sale of thousands of sheep. The population was largely illiterate and devoutly Moslem. They were strictly proscribed from eating pork or anything contaminated by association with pork. Then and now, True Believers allow themselves to be manipulated by the unwise and the unscrupulous.

Father told me that he would have to meet with the caliph to sort things out. It would take several hours, so he gave me a few dollars and told me to enjoy myself. I explored the city for awhile, then ended up in a cabaret, a bar / restaurant, where I was quickly surrounded by several women intent on showing me a good time. They plied me with their attentions and alcohol. I felt very flattered and grownup.

Meanwhile Father had finished with the caliph. Like two sensible businessmen, then had struck a deal. For a fee, the caliph would deny the rumors of sheep suckling on pigs' milk so that Father could sell the sheep.

But, I was not waiting for Father back at our hotel. He walked the business district, looking everywhere, then began to worry. Finally, he contacted the police and they searched the city. The police eventually located me, passed out drunk in the street, in nothing but my underwear.

Father brought me a change of clothing, and we headed back to the hotel. My memory of his reaction is a bit cloudy, except for one remark he made. "Have you learned anything from this?" he asked.

"Yes, Father," I replied. "I learned never to let ladies swindle me again."

He nodded his approval.

I found myself pondering that long-ago lesson as I allowed one of the bar signs in Covington to draw me into an "all-nude" show. I sat through it while sipping exorbitantly-priced drinks, while a lovely lady sat with me and encouraged me to buy her drinks. "I enjoy your company and would be glad to have you sit here," I told her. "I'll even buy you drinks. But, don't treat me like a sucker."

There was a stimulating raw energy to the performance and the bar itself. I imagined the patrons to be "respectable" Cincinnatians here for a fix of passion missing from their lives. They were nearly as interesting to watch as the show. But most interesting of all were the women who worked there.

I liked Covington and visited often. I had a few favorite bars where I became known. I was a scientist studying this social phenomenon, I would joke to the women there and to myself. In truth, it was a pleasant enough diversion in its own right.

I got to know the women. I tipped them well so that they would not have to hustle me for watered-down drinks. I became less of a customer and more of an acquaintance. There in the din of the bar and the strip show, they would share carefully chosen bits about their lives. Sometimes, they were young and pretty, ambitious for better things. Sometimes the desperateness of a hard life had lined their face before its time, and they had settled into a somber acceptance of what life had handed them.

* * *

What is it like in Covington? " Father Leahy asked me one day. "Is it as sinful as people say?"

"More sinful than you can imagine," I said. "That's why I go there."

Every so often he would ask me again about Covington, until finally he decided that he should go there himself.

"A priest in Covington?" I said.

"If I am to counsel the boys about that place and the temptation of its vices, I should know what it's like."

So, I agreed to be his guide. On the appointed night, he showed up at my apartment with two other priests from the Xavier faculty, all neatly dressed in suits. Covington was a short drive from Cincinnati but a great moral distance from the hallowed halls of Xavier. Wide-eyed, my priestly companions craned their necks at all the signs promising the lurid shows inside the various bars and clubs. I imagined them feeling like Dante in *The Divine Comedy*, being led into Hell by the poet Virgil, passing beneath a sign which read "Abandon all hope ye who enter here."

At one of my favorite bars, I set them up at a table and then went to speak to the woman in charge. "Here's half of a twenty," I said. I tore a twenty dollar bill in half before her nose. "If you send three of your best girls over to be very friendly to those men over there, I'll give you the other half." She agreed. "However," I added, "the girls should not touch me, just the men in suits."

Shortly, the women appeared. They wore short skirts, tight-fitting tops, and much makeup, and they pretended to find these three stiff men in suits irresistible. They rubbed against them, sat in their laps, and ran fingers through their hair, and started touching them all over. I had never seen quite the deep shade of red that colored the priests' faces that night.

Although they were profoundly uncomfortable, I imagined that on another level, they enjoyed holding out against temptation. Like Christ resisting Satan in the wilderness, they proved the strength of their faith by holding firm against temptation. Of course, they were only men and they had their limits. Before too long, they asked to leave.

Silence filled the car as we drove back towards Cincinnati. What must be running through those priestly minds, I wondered. Temptation of the flesh is a powerful force, even for the godly. I hoped that I had seriously corrupted them.

Finally, Father Leahy spoke in his usual ministerial tone of voice. "Mark, did you happen to notice that the women were friendly only to the three of us and not to you? Are we so handsome, or what?" I assured him that was the case.

Perhaps it was Father Leahy's wish to mend my errant ways that caused him to one day suggest, "Mark, you are a good fellow. Why don't you become a Catholic?"

"Father, in my religion there are no sins. If I became a Catholic that same day I'd be the greatest sinner in the world."

He laughed at the logic of my position and agreed that both I and Catholicism would be better off if I did not join the faith. We continued to be good friends, each accepting the fact that the other was not likely to change his ways.

Meanwhile, I felt restless about my life. I was enormously busy, teaching full time at one college and part time at another college. But Mount Saint Joseph felt like a dead end for me. Where was my life going? my career? Christina visited me occasionally; more often I drove back to Toronto for a weekend visit. We had been dating for several years by then, lovers and friends, but no more. I was 36 years old, but my life seemed too unsettled to think about marriage.

About this time, I met a fellow Romanian immigrant, a former lawyer, teaching at the University of Cincinnati. We had a lot in common and became close friends. He was dating an older wealthy woman. "She wants to get married," he told me.

"Marry her," I advised. He rolled his head. Like me he enjoyed being single. In Romania, men often married late in life, when they had established themselves, and then they took young wives. There was the recent example in the news of former first lady, Jackie Kennedy, marrying a much older man, Greek shipping magnate Aristotle Onassis.

My friend and I never articulated our marriage philosophy, but if we had, it would have followed that scenario. We would drift into middle age, settle securely into a career, and then think about marriage, home, and family.

My friend decided against marrying his rich, older woman at about the same time my heart was being stolen by a young novice at Mount Saint Joseph. It was her breathtaking beauty that attracted me. She took one of my classes, dressed in her novice uniform of black and white, which only emphasized her beauty all the more. What a waste to commit such loveliness to the sisterhood.

My turn to be tempted, with this forbidden fruit. But unlike my holy friends, I embraced my human weaknesses. I was not a god but a man, not like Christ but like Adam, surrendering to the temptations of Eve.

The term infatuation is not quite strong enough to describe the hold she took on my imagination. I anticipated my class solely for the opportunity to gaze upon her, and had to guard myself against being too distracted during lectures. She was constantly in my thoughts, and I plotted ways to get to know her. I had never before been so totally under the sway of a woman. Her name was Helen.

Eventually, we started having conferences in my office to discuss the class and sociology in general. The chemistry of our mutual attraction seemed a palpable force urging us together, but stronger forces resisted that attraction. She was, after all, promised to Christ. When we embraced and kissed on one occasion, I could feel the tension within her. She did not show up for the next class. Nor the next. I began to worry. Had I rushed her? Had I pushed too far?

When she did not appear after two weeks, I finally asked the Mother Superior about Helen. "Do not worry about, Helen," she snapped. "She is none of your concern." There was the answer to my question. The good novice that she was, Helen had confessed our kiss, perhaps her own struggle between desire and her vows. The result was that Helen was transferred away from the Mount, and I never saw her again. My Eve exiled from the Garden.

Of course, I too did not want to stay at the Mount any longer than necessary. The religious environment had begun to chafe. It seemed so restrictive, so out of touch with reality, so incapable of preparing these girls for the real struggles they would face in life. It had served its purpose for me, getting me out of Toronto and launching my career as a professor, but now I wanted to move on.

Eager to get my life back on track and further my career, I applied to the doctoral program at the University of Cincinnati. To my surprise, I was turned down. "We received a scathing letter from the Department Chair in Toronto," they explained to me. "What did you do, murder his father?" Hilliard was making good on his promise that I would never earn my doctorate anywhere. Obviously, he personally would see to that.

So, I settled in for another year of teaching at Mount Saint Joseph.

By my second year at the Mount, I had well established myself as an outsider. Since I did not appear at Mass, nor espouse religious doctrine in class, I was clearly distinct from the sisters. Perhaps being a foreigner also suggested that I was worldly and more accepting of matters that would have troubled the nuns.

Regardless of the cause, I developed an excellent rapport with students. They enjoyed visiting my office to talk. Problems with roommates, boyfriends, or parents occupied them. But so did the conflict between their normal adolescent interests and the restrictive environment of the school. The problems were often petty, but sometimes more serious.

I can't recall those times without bringing to mind the face of a girl named Molly. She sat in my office, stiff and nervous with some secret that needed telling. A friend had recommended that she speak with me, she explained. "Something has happened, and I don't know what to do." I had learned that with these students, such a remark might only preface the disclosure of some petty offense, such as missing curfew or arguments with the nuns.

But Molly wrestled mightily with what she was about to tell me before speaking the truth very softly, "I'm pregnant." The confession came with a burst of tears. It was the worst thing. Her life was over. I assured her that it wasn't.

"Yes it is," she insisted. She'd be expelled from school. Her parents? She didn't even want to think about that. "It's even worse than you think," she said. "They wouldn't understand." I waited through more tears while she built up the courage to go on. "He was . . . a Negro," she whispered.

Whether in fact she had become pregnant by a black man, I couldn't say. That may have been a story she thought would shock me into helping her. Because it had become obvious that she had come to me for one reason.

She wanted an abortion, wanted someone to suggest such a thing, wanted to believe herself that her problem had an easy solution. Abortions were not so easily come by in those days, and for a good catholic student at Mount St. Joseph to be considering it was a ticket to Hell.

I tried to be as comforting and objective as I could. But, of course, I knew that she was right to imagine that her future would be dramatically altered by a pregnancy. So, I mentioned the word that she wouldn't have heard whispered anywhere else in that institution—abortion. It was an alternative. If that's what she wanted, I would see if I could assist her.

It had a very obvious appeal for her. "I've thought about that," she said with great seriousness. "But, I couldn't. It's a mortal sin."

I could list my arguments against religion, go on for pages and pages, but none struck me as more compelling at that moment than its ability to ruin this girl's life. I felt an anger swell inside me against Catholicism in general, and in particular against Mount Saint Joseph and all the pious pretensions of the place and its strict religious teachings.

I called my friend Father Phillip, the campus priest, to explain the situation. He had always impressed me as a realist and he didn't disappoint me now. I sent Molly to speak with him, and he gave her absolution to have the abortion. We saw ourselves as working in collaboration to save this girl from the nuns.

Later Father Phillip would leave the priesthood and marry. I suspect I was a bad influence on him.

As the end of my second year at the Mount approached, plans were under way on campus for Parents' Day festivities. This was a chance for the nuns to show off their new buildings and beautiful campus, and a chance for the students to have some fun.

There would be a carnival, with a midway and lots of games. I was recruited to be the gypsy fortune teller. In preparation, several of the girls told me secrets about their classmates, things that no one else knew. They were largely innocent, adolescent rebellions—disobedience to the rules of parents or school, experiments with alcohol and sex. On the day of the big event, I played my part to the hilt. Dressed like a gypsy in my little booth, I received my visitors, gazed into my crystal ball, and amazed them with my knowledge of their darkest secrets. If I did not have information on a student, I would complain that the moon was not right to read her fortune.

This would have been great fun if I had stopped at that, but not for the first or last time, my mouth got me into trouble. It seems that no amount of bad experience was capable of teaching me this lesson.

All my resentment against Mount Joseph's and my having to be a part of its religious environment, had been building inside me. It vented itself on this occasion in an offhand remark. The mood was relaxed. The handsome campus brimmed with affluent parents, proud of their daughters, pleased with themselves for having chosen a fine religious school like Mount Saint Joseph for their child's education. I was so struck by the irony of the moment, with all those secret indiscretions floating around my head, that I made a comment to some parents. "You pay $6,000 for tuition, and your daughters still lose their virginity." The college president, Sister Mary Grace called me in the next day to tell me I was fired. My response was, "I quit!"

Although I had met some good students and friends there, I did not mourn the loss of my job at Mount Saint Joseph. The fit had never been right. It was late in the year to be launching a job search, but, fortunately, sociologists were still in demand and openings existed. In short order I had five interviews lined up.

The first interview took me to Edinboro State College, in Edinboro, Pennsylvania. They had a fledgling sociology program that had been cobbled together with faculty from other disciplines and social scientists whose highest academic achievement was a Master's Degree from Edinboro. They wanted a researcher, and I fit the bill. Following my interview, the dean offered me the job and insisted on an answer on the spot. Although I had other interviews lined up, I accepted the offer. Edinboro had $20,000 to underwrite research, and that very much appealed to me.

"I'll stay for two years," I told the dean.

Twenty-nine years later, I'm still there.

12
Another Home

At the crest of the hill, I pulled my car to the side of the street, got out and stared northward. Stretching beneath me was the city of Erie, Pennsylvania, where I had just taken an apartment. Shortly after I had moved here, I saw an advertisement in the newspaper from a local hotel, claiming that it was the "liveliest night spot in Erie." I paid a visit, only to find a near-empty ballroom in a run-down hotel. Two women shuffled across the floor, dancing together. "If this is the liveliest night spot in Erie," I said to myself, "then I'm in trouble."

From my vantage point on that hill I could see a peaceful bay embracing the city shoreline, and beyond that the expanse of Lake Erie. I had been told that on a clear day, you could see Canada across the lake as a thin grey line on the horizon.

I squinted hard into the distance. Shades of blue mottled the waters. Mist clouded the far skyline. Some dark form lay out there, but whether it was Ontario or a trick of light and shadows, I couldn't tell.

I was beginning to feel like quite the nomad. After seven years in North America, I had lived at four locations in two different countries, not counting a few on-site research stints in the far north. That trend would continue for the next few years.

I had begun teaching at Edinboro State College, 20 miles south of Erie. Their fledgling sociology program needed much help. Although they had hired me as a researcher, I was once again kept busy creating many new courses, courses in theory and methodology, but also in criminology, delinquency, even industrial organization. Another temporary appointment, I told myself. Make the most of it.

Every institution has its own culture and its own cast of characters that give it a distinctive atmosphere. Edinboro in those years was trying to change its image from that of a "teaching college" to more of a serious university. Edinboro's dean was an curmudgeonly old fellow named Luther Hendricks, known to the faculty as "the bear." Not only was he the dean, but he also served as acting chair of whatever department was temporarily chairless. He wielded considerable power.

Hendricks had recruited me because he thought I could be a high-profile faculty member, doing research and publishing to draw attention to Edinboro and give credibility to its sociology department. And that is what I set about doing. I conducted a study in ethnic stereotyping, and another study on the value orientation of students, faculty, and parents regarding their perception of a university. I wrote a theoretical paper on an approach to evaluating social phenomena and began a series of research projects for the Pennsylvania Criminal Justice Commission that studied victimization. This is what my education and training had prepared me to do. It was nice to be at an institution that valued my work.

Or, so I thought. I was surprised one day to find an angry letter to the editor in the campus newspaper about me. It appeared that not everyone was happy that I was doing research. The letter criticized me for promoting a publish-or-perish mentality, which would corrupt the pure teaching function of the faculty.

Was I undermining the teaching mission of the college? My initial reaction was that it is impossible to teach a course in research methods unless you engage in research. Of course, different colleges place different emphasis on research and teaching, requiring a heavier or lighter teaching load depending on their expectations for research or publications. But I have always felt that a faculty member must stay fully involved with his or her discipline.

I never wrote a rebuttal to that letter, but if I had it probably would have conceded that a mindless emphasis on publishing *can* undermine the time and effort it takes to be an effective teacher. And there is certainly an ocean of worthless academic writing being published that serves little purpose other than to put professors in print.

On the other hand, when research and publication is not valued, professors can lose touch with their field. They can become downright lazy. This is far more common than most would like to believe: professors who deliver lectures from twenty-year-old notes, who do not read the current literature, and who consider a speech at the Rotary Club, an appearance on local television, or a letter in the newspaper as a demonstration of their academic competence.

Whereas the resentment of a few faculty members didn't affect my functioning on campus, the conflict that developed with "The Bear" certainly did. Hendricks had been at Edinboro so long, operating as the institution's benevolent parent, that he took offense when professors did not offer him parental obedience. He expected everyone's compliance on matters of curriculum and policy. Questions raised his ire. Challenges earned his open hostility.

Unfortunately, it is not my way to dissemble. If I did not agree with Hendricks, I told him so. If I thought an issue would benefit from a frank discussion, I initiated it. Before long our disagreements erupted into open arguments. After one particularly bitter exchange, I ordered him out of my office. As a consequence, I became *persona non grata*. I was banned from attending meetings. The phone was removed from my office one day, the bookshelves the next. I felt under siege. Colleagues began to avoid me because of my pariah status.

Hendricks was punishing me for questioning his authority. I had been too honest, too confrontational, and was paying the price. This was a problem that I had faced on numerous occasions in my life. Was I simply unable to work with any authority figure or was there a particular quality of certain authority figures that triggered this response in me?

A number of factors contributed to the problem situation on this occasion, not the least of which was the personalities of the individuals involved. Hendricks had gotten his way at Edinboro for so long, that he governed with supreme authority. Whereas for me, it was that old, devil streak of stubbornness once again leading me into trouble. I credit my dear mother for this. Sometimes I imagine my parents as two warring sides of my personality. Mother is the strong, unyielding oak tree, rigid with her own convictions and values. Father is the inveterate pragmatist, the resourceful palm tree finding sustenance on the most barren soil, bending before the strongest wind. He was inventive and adaptive, always ready to strike a compromise, to negotiate a deal. The challenge for me was to use the appropriate parental role model in the appropriate situation.

Fortunately, at Edinboro, there were enough good-quality students to make my teaching rewarding, despite the atmosphere of tension. I was very demanding, and they accepted the challenge of hard work to learn the discipline. In one methodology course I taught with 14 students, five went on to earn their Ph.D.s, and four got their Masters.

I had not abandoned my own desire to finish work on my Ph'D. When I applied to Case Western Reserve University, I cautioned them, "If you contact the University of Toronto, they'll tell you I'm the worst person in the world." Thankfully, they did not contact Toronto, and I was accepted into their doctoral program.

I had completed much of the course work for my doctorate at the University of Toronto. Yet when I told my advisor at Case Western that I wanted to earn my Ph.D. in one year, he was incredulous. "It took me *ten* years to get my degree."

"But I have to earn a living," I told him.

What a blur that time seems to me now. The image recalled is one of speeding along at 100 mph on the highway between Cleveland and Edinboro, racing back and forth from classes at Case and teaching at Edinboro with scarcely a minute to breathe. I was impatient on the highway and with the circumstances. Case Western was being very understanding of my circumstances, but in a sense, I was earning my doctorate a second time. Although I had not yet taken my preliminary exams, I had begun work on my dissertation. Every spare moment of my busy schedule was devoted to writing the dissertation, which made a comparison between the position of the French-speaking people I had studied in Canada and American blacks.

When it came time to defend my dissertation, my advisor warned that a black professor on my committee might give me a hard time because the material I had used about blacks was not gathered firsthand. I came to the meeting with my committee lugging two suitcases. The professors joked: Was I planning a trip? Was I skipping town? I gave no explanation.

I knew that my research was solid. I had done all the primary research on the French-speaking population and used an exhaustive list of the latest secondary sources to make the comparison to blacks. When the complaint came that I had expected, the professor charged that I did not know enough about the black experience to have made the comparison.

That was when I opened the suitcases. They were filled with books and articles. "Here, are the experts I relied upon," I said, tossing them onto the table in front of my committee. "If I am wrong, then all of them are wrong as well."

When they had finished with me, I was asked to wait outside for their decision. In a short while, my advisor appeared. "Mark, you are crazy. But your dissertation was accepted."

Odd, this character trait I possess that makes me abandon self-interest in the face of such obstacles as bureaucracy, deceit, or stupidity. Despite my behavior before the committee, I passed my defense and earned my doctorate.

In hindsight, the blur of activity from my time at Case Western strikes me as both a literal and a figurative image. I logged more miles than I care to remember in those years.

But, all of society raced along at break neck speed in the late 1960s. Not that I was a stranger to dramatic change. Few people can boast of having lived under monarchy, fascism, Communism, and democracy. Change has been the dominant theme in my life and being adaptive one of my most vital survival strategies.

So, I took in stride most of the counter-culture issues that came to the fore in those years. I sympathized with the views of the younger generation on such issues as Civil Rights and equality of the sexes. On only one issue did I find myself in dramatic opposition to the prevailing views of the young—the war in Vietnam.

For me that war came down to one simple yet critical issue: opposition to the spread of Communism. Like few others who entered the debate in those years, I spoke from experience. I knew the complacency that settles over a population in the face of the advance of a brutal regime. I had lived it. I had watched as the influence of the Iron Guard grew so pervasive in Romania, watched again as the justifications were trotted out for our alliance with Nazi Germany, and watched a third time as the brutal measures of the Communists quieted opposition and established their reign of terror and repression.

I won the praise of some faculty when I wrote a letter to the campus newspaper supporting U.S. involvement in Southeast Asia, claiming that the same arguments that justified our opposition to the Nazis in Europe applied to our opposition to the communists in Vietnam. Occasionally, during my years as an immigrant, I had thought Americans naive about politics. They were too apathetic, too untutored in the ways of oppression. I felt compelled to raise my voice about such things and became the resident hawk at Edinboro and wherever I found an audience. "I know Communism," I would tell them, "I have lived under repressive governments. With them you don't compromise and you don't placate. They will accept what you give them, then take by force whatever else you have. You don't accept their rhetoric of world brotherhood; it is the slogan of enslavement."

This was not a popular message on college campuses during the late 1960s. I was once invited to debate the issue in Toronto with a speaker from Berkeley. He spoke first to enthusiastic applause. When my turn came, I was pelted with tomatoes and eggs, and left the stage without even the opportunity to present my view. They could not have invented a better demonstration of oppression. The country was weary of war. It is easy to weary of a war you are not winning.

In fact, that was my only complaint about the war. The United States was the most powerful nation on earth, and it was not using its full power to win in Vietnam. It seemed to lack the will to win. It is better not to use power at all than to use it wrongly. Therefore, I supported not simply a continuation of the war, but an escalation. On this issue, I favored the radical views of Senator and presidential candidate Barry Goldwater, who advocated dropping the atomic bomb on North Vietnam.

Of course, much of my attitude towards Vietnam was personal, sentimental. I did believe we had to halt the spread of Communism. But whenever the subject came up, I experienced a visceral rather than a logical reaction. My blood pressure skyrocketed, opening flood gates of rage from half a life ago. Some anti-war supporter might have showered me with an incredibly logical argument why the U.S. should leave Vietnam, and it would not have penetrated my hatred for Communism. After all, his argument would have been only theory and abstraction, but my conviction wore a face.

I could see the face of Georgi, the young student who joined the partisans to fight the Communists; the face of my childhood friend, Emil, transformed to a monster by high position in the Party, the face of Secretary Ceausescu when I refused his request to edit the newspaper, the faces of my parents when they were forced to leave their only child behind in a country they had once loved then loathed and feared, the thousand faces of the lost men of Pereprava, and the million vacant faces of citizens on the streets of Bucharest. Do not spout political theory to me. I have looked Communism square in the eye, and I tell you it is evil, as evil as the worst creations of the Nazis.

I never spoke my feelings about the war in those terms, but that was the bitter knot of emotions that lay at the heart of my support for the war in Vietnam.

*   *   *

My good friend and dissertation advisor at Case Western Reserve, Victor Thiessen, stopped by my office one day, waving a letter in my face. "Want to teach at the University of Alabama in Huntsville?" A colleague at the U of A had written to say that they were looking to hire a team of sociologists capable of conducting research and developing the department. I didn't hesitate a second. The time I had spent at Case Western Reserve had given me an invigorating taste of what it was like to work among talented colleagues, at an institution that valued and encouraged research. We would have to visit Alabama for an interview, Thiessen explained.

A few days before we left, I was contacted by a student at Edinboro who had heard I was heading for Alabama and wanted a ride as far as Columbus, OH. Her name was Joyce Miller. She was a sociology major who had taken many courses from me.

She came to Cleveland the night before our departure, and the four of us visited a favorite restaurant, the Hungarian Village. The owner was a good friend with old-world notions of hospitality. We stayed on after the restaurant closed to drink with him. When the mood was liberally mellowed with drink, the owner broke out his violin and filled the empty restaurant with ballads and folk songs. I was inspired to take the microphone and croon some old Romanian songs. Joyce joined us on piano, and before long we had a regular concert going.

There is a special chemistry to moments like that. You let your hair down with friends or strangers, and you instantly feel closer to them. You have seen each other exposed. I remember being aware of Joyce in a different way that night. It was the beginning of a relationship that soon led to dating and romance.

The following day we dropped Joyce off in Columbus and continued on to Alabama as the potential "team" of professors. The situation at the University of Alabama looked very attractive. The sociology department was new, with ambitious plans for development. We would be hired at a salary roughly twice what I was currently earning. Generous grants were available for research, and there would be the opportunity for interesting and lucrative consulting work with the federal government in Huntsville. We needed no additional convincing that we should come to Alabama, but the department decided to throw a party in our honor. It was a party that will forever live in my memory.

I can't recall what we expected of a faculty party, probably something very stuffy, with the usual cast of academics and spouses sipping white wine and exchanging cocktail chatter. Instead, a woman passing by in her underwear signaled that our expectations would be very off the mark.

The year was 1970, deep into the hard-driving era of counter culture, with its sex, drugs, and rock and roll. Apparently, the U of A had embraced the counter culture with a vengeance. Rock music buzzed insistently in the background. Alcohol was still the drug of choice. And sex? The concept of inhibition did not exist at that party. Like initiates at a bacchanal, we were swept up in the action.

On the drive back home the next day, the three of us were still shaking our heads. Did that really happen? Had we really attended that party? None of us were Puritans, but we had never encountered anything like that.

When Alabama extended us a job offer, my colleagues were hesitant about leaving secure positions at Case Western. To me, the opportunity looked too good to pass up. We agreed that I would accept the position. If it turned out to be as good as it looked, the other two would come to Alabama the following year. I decided to play it safe myself by taking an official leave of absence from Edinboro. I would be a visiting professor at the University of Alabama. If things worked out, I too would make the move official at a later date.

Once again the nomad, I moved to Huntsville. The University of Alabama was a stimulating place to work, and I settled quickly into a routine of teaching and research. Not long after I arrived there, I was contacted by Joyce Miller. She had graduated from Edinboro and was looking for work. When I found her a position in the university's computer department, she moved to Huntsville.

We began to see a lot of each other.

* * *

When I answered the knock at the door of my apartment in Huntsville, Alabama, a man greeted me by displaying a badge that identified him as an agent of the FBI.

"May I have a few words with you?" he asked, and I invited him in.

In a flash, I was back in Bucharest, opening the door to the secret police agents who hauled me away to Pereprava. The memory was instantly vivid in my mind, the old suspicions and fears crowding my chest.

"Who's there?" a voice called from upstairs. It was Joyce.

"It is FBI policy," he explained, "to conduct an investigation of an individual whenever that person is accused of being a spy."

Accused of being a spy? What was he talking about? A knife edge of panic cut into my imagination. I knew that I had done nothing wrong and that I was in the United States, not Romania. But, still . . . a spy?

"Mark, who's there?" Joyce called out again.

"Excuse me for a moment," I said to the agent, and went upstairs. "It's the FBI, and they think I'm a spy," I whispered to Joyce. "Sit at the top of the stairs and listen to the conversation."

The situation became clearer when I returned downstairs and the agent continued. The FBI had received information from someone implicating me as a spy. They were required to investigate all such charges.

"But, that's ridiculous," I said.

He shrugged as if to suggest that anything was possible in his world. "We have had you under careful surveillance ever since then," he said, "including tapping your telephone."

I didn't know whether to be angry or scared. To whom had I spoken on the phone? How many unguarded things had I revealed? There had been calls to girlfriends and colleagues. I had been doing research for a government agency in Huntsville, which was supposed to be secret, but had never mentioned any of that on the phone. I didn't know what to think.

"Whenever we conclude such an investigation," the agent continued, "we always visit the individual involved. So, I am here simply to tell you that we have closed the investigation and found no truth to the charge."

"You mean I am not Mata Hari?"

"It doesn't look that way. Although, I can say that . . . you're living one incredibly wild life."

When the agent left, Joyce came down from upstairs. Joyce had come to live in Huntsville after her college graduation when I had arranged a job for her. Our relationship had quickly developed into a serious romance. She looked a bit shaken at that moment. She had come a long way quickly from undergraduate days at Edinboro State College and a small-town upbringing in Youngstown, Ohio.

Now she was romantically involved with foreigner who had been accused of spying. We were able to joke about it, but for a long time, I speculated about who had charged me with spying. Some Romanian in Winnipeg or Toronto? Perhaps some recent immigrant from Communist Romania being debriefed by the CIA had dropped my name? Someone at Edinboro State College? I never learned the identity of my accuser, though I'm convinced that they did it not for any concern for national security but for personal spite.

Not long after that incident I presented myself at the immigration office in Birmingham to become an American citizen. I had previously made one such visit in Pittsburgh and been offended when they asked me ridiculous questions to establish my literacy. "What is this?" the clerk had asked, holding up a pencil. "A pencil," I responded warily. "What is this?" she held up a pen.

"What are you doing? I asked.

"We need to see if you understand English."

"I have a Ph.D. from an American university!" I insisted. But that didn't matter, I had to answer the stupid questions. I walked out, enraged that they would automatically assume that immigrants lacked a basic education or intelligence. This was a stereotype not only of the Immigration and Naturalization Service, but of much of society. I had encountered it in many guises over the years. Lesson: People have preconceived notions about immigrants, often negative. Learn to anticipate them. Learn to deal with them. Even today, the stereotype persists.

I ran into no such hurdle in Birmingham. They assumed that a professor, holding a Ph.D. from an American university, must have mastered a basic command of English. So, in 1970, I became a citizen of the United States of America.

It felt like I was entering another phase of my life, as though circumstances were lining up to push me in a new direction. A decade after leaving Romania, I had become an official citizen of another country. I had reached 40 years of age. And love had entered my life in the person of Joyce Miller. We had begun to talk about marriage. I had resolved that now was the time in my life, and this was the person with whom to take the plunge.

However, Joyce did not like the atmosphere at Alabama. She very much wanted us to return to Edinboro so that she could begin work on her own Ph.D. at some university in the region. I wrote to Edinboro, informing them that I had a signed contract from Alabama but wished to return that fall. I received a letter from the vice president informing me that if I returned, it would be at my old salary of $12,300, plus I would never receive promotion. They did not promote people who worked.

I suppose this was an allusion to my many research projects, or more likely a spiteful consequence of my strained relations with the administration. I swallowed hard on that one, frustrated that I would be leaving such a rich and nurturing environment at Alabama, where I was earning more than twice the salary that Edinboro promised, for Edinboro's provincial attitude and its special brand of academic politics.

But, my life was filling with other things in those years. Back in Erie, Pennsylvania in 1971, Joyce Miller and I married in a very brief ceremony at the office of a justice of the peace. We settled into a house near Edinboro, Joyce began her graduate schooling, and I continued doing research for the Governor's Justice Commission in the areas of delinquency and criminal offenses and sentencing.

It had taken a long time for me to marry. My notions about marriage had evolved as a blend of Old World / European attitudes and the more liberal attitudes of America in the 1970s. Now, I was 42 years old, marrying a much younger woman.

The love that I felt drew me wonderfully close to Joyce, and yet in some ways I felt worlds apart from her. Was it a combination of age, cultural differences, education, worldliness? She was so young. She had grown up in Youngstown, Ohio and had never traveled more than a few hundred miles from home. She had grown up in America in the 1950s and 1960s, an era of political stability and unbroken economic prosperity. Could the personality of such a woman ever meld with my own?

In those early years, I thought to expand her horizons and increase her awareness of the larger world. I planned to expose her to new ideas and stimulating friends, encourage her academic ambitions, and travel abroad with her to experience foreign cultures. All of which would bring us closer, in a more substantive way. We would share ideas, opinions, dreams.

I followed through on much of that, though in reality it didn't take long before the influence flowed two ways. She encouraged me, exposed me to new friends and ideas, and gave me an insider's perspective on my adopted culture. We would collaborate on research projects, and she would convince me to establish an independent research organization.

However, no matter how close we became, how much of an equal footing we achieved, there would always remain a gap in our relationship. To characterize it as a European versus an American value orientation is something of an over simplification, but it comes close to reality. How much of it is also a factor of difference in our life experiences, not even a psychiatrist could determine.

* * *

My research projects from the State Justice Commission were funneled through my employer Edinboro State College. As the administrative unit overseeing the work, they received a 10 percent administrative fee. It was Joyce who finally pointed out to me that I was receiving nothing from Edinboro for that 10 percent. They did not assist in acquiring the grants, nor provide secretarial or equipment support.

"Why not start your own research organization," Joyce suggested, "and get some use from that 10 percent?" It was an inspired idea, a mark of the confidence and boldness taking root in Joyce's character. I recruited a handful of friends to be my board of directors, and in 1975 established the Northwest Institute of Research, a fancy name for the tiny office in my home.

But one other event occurred prior to that which seemed to put a close on a chapter of my life. A letter arrived from Silviu, my long-time friend from Romania. Silviu, a Party member, had had a good position in communications in Romania. But he too had finally soured on the Communist government and made his escape. For a year he had waited in Italy for a visa. Now, he had arrived in Toronto, and he invited me to come see him.

I drove up for the reunion of two old friends. He got to meet Joyce. I got to hear about his life in Romania and his escape. Marconi, the Canadian communications firm had recruited him for a job as soon he stepped from the plane.

Forty years had passed since we had been school boys in Braila. So many great machinations of war and politics had intervened to shape our lives. Of the four school chums who had first met in Catholic primary school during the innocent pre-war years in Braila, Romania, Ion had become a soldier and emigrated to Israel. Emil had pursued power and had lost a bit of his soul to it during his time in high Party office. At last report, he had become a respected professor of art history in Romania.

Silviu and Mark sat across from each other in a Toronto apartment and toasted to each other's good fortune.

13
Visiting Professor in Pakistan

I sat at the desk in the front of the classroom as it filled with the faculty members who would be my students. They eyed me with intense curiosity; some smiled or gave a discreet nod. When they had filled the desks and opened notebooks, they looked eagerly in my direction to see what this American had to say to them.

I was at Sind University in Pakistan, once again a visiting professor. It was as much the spirit of adventure as the opportunity for new professional experience that had sent me here in 1975. The opportunity arose out of my friendship with a Pakistani professor teaching at Edinboro, who mentioned that Pakistani universities needed American professors. Through him I arranged for a year of teaching at Sind University.

This year abroad would also be an opportunity for Joyce to "see the world," something beyond the narrow confines of geography and thought in Middle America. When the academic year ended, we would travel in Europe and also visit Romania. I had no burning desire to revisit my homeland, but Joyce was curious.

Despite a cordial reception, it was easy to feel like an outsider in Pakistan, where culture and religion were so foreign to my experience. The English language remained in many parts of the country as an artifact of British rule. It was the language spoken at the University. But religion and custom had a way of ambushing our best intentions.

The university chancellor had said that his faculty needed instruction in how to conduct research, so here I was on my first day, set to teach research methodology to a room full of Pakistani professors.

Mindful of cultural differences, wary of inadvertently broaching some rule of etiquette, I took my time with personal introductions and then led slowly into an explanation of the course. When I had finished a basic explanation of the scientific method, I asked for questions. The Dean of Liberal Arts was taking the course, sitting as a commanding presence in the front of the room. His hand shot up immediately.

"That is not true," he said.

"What do you mean?" I asked.

"What you have said about the scientific method determining the truth."

"I'm not talking about finding the truth," I said, "merely arriving at a possible *explanation*. That's better than ignorance."

Explanation and truth are not found in research but in the *Koran*."

A roomful of quizzical faces sharpened their focus on me, waiting for my response. If any of them had contrary opinions, they were not about to contradict their dean. I felt as though I had blundered into a cultural mine field. It did not take me long to realize the implications of his statement. It literally undercut the entire basis for the course, which explored the scientific approach to gathering information and developing an explanation for phenomena. In the minds of those professors, truth was an article of faith, not of scientific discovery.

I gathered my lecture notes, stuffed them into a folder, and marched straight to the office of the chancellor. He understood the problem. We settled on a new assignment for me, helping the university to establish a research institute. I was glad for this new task. Having just created my own research institute at home, I knew how to go about it. More or less. Now I would try to do it in Pakistan.

My only question for the chancellor, "How was an institute to conduct research if it violated the teachings of the *Koran*?" It would not be a problem, he assured me. He had already concluded that the problem was less with the *Koran*, than with the Dean. Which was the case. For the balance of my stay there, tension existed between the Dean and me. He saw me as a contaminating force.

The pervasiveness and power of the Moslem faith flowed as an undercurrent beneath all of life at Sind. Behaviors and attitudes that might have been viewed as part of their culture, were, for some Pakistanis, part of their faith. Of course, this tension existed not only between Pakistanis and foreign visitors, but among Pakistanis themselves. A tide of fundamentalism had appeared in Moslem countries, aggravating the conflict between the faith and the forces of modernization. A charismatic fundamentalist, the Ayatollah Khomeini, had been expelled from Iran because his influence threatened the social order.

It's worth pausing here to say a few words about Sind University and Pakistani academic life. Sind University was located in the desert, on an expanse of barren land. The nearest town, Hyderabad, was about ten miles away. Approximately 60 miles to the south, on the Arabian Sea, stood Karachi, the provincial capital.

An odd mixture of class and caste governed behavior. Every faculty member's office contained a buzzer. With the push of a button, you could summon a servant to bring you afternoon tea or fetch you a newspaper.

One of the customs less easily accommodated regarded attitudes towards women. As in other Moslem countries, Pakistani women were kept in the background, figuratively and literally. Every activity was segregated by the sexes. Though the University faculty included some women, they had their own lounge. I would sometimes stop in there and be well received. I think they thought it a refreshingly liberal attitude that a man would want to pass time with them.

While Joyce and I generally tried to show respect for Pakistani customs, this one seemed too contrary to our own beliefs to adopt. At social gatherings, where men and women would meet in separate rooms, Joyce would spend some time with the women, then join the men.

It raised a few eyebrows, but eventually the Pakistani men made their own adjustment to our behavior. Not that we had struck some great blow for feminism. The Pakistani men had not changed their attitudes towards women, simply changed their attitudes towards Joyce. They had simply redefined her as "one of the boys," a token, and temporary, shift in their perspective to get them through this abnormal situation.

Still, throughout our stay, our servant, who was our resident expert on local custom, had to keep Joyce alert to possible dangers. Whether socializing at the University or on our extensive travels around the country, he would always be reminding her of possible danger. Not a danger of offending custom, but of eliciting unwanted behavior from men. If a woman wore slacks, displayed too much skin, or traveled alone, she was sending certain signals and putting herself into possibly dangerous situations.

Joyce and I argued occasionally about that. She might feel no compunction about acting with all the freedom of an American woman, but we were in Pakistan, and the reality was that she would not simply be displaying modern western female behavior, but literally exposing herself to danger.

This lesson between theory and reality was one I too would learn as I began the job of creating a research institute. Sind University had never before gotten research money from the federal government. In Islamabad I presented my proposal to the Director of Grants. He was impressed with the thoroughness and feasibility of my plan and granted us "start-up" money. Back at the university, they were delighted. A research institute would give them great credibility within the national education system. I was given the green light to make it happen.

* * *

One day there was a knock on the door of our bungalow, and who should be standing there but my old friend Silviu. What a surprise to run into him in Pakistan. He was on assignment for his employer, Marconi, to set up a new communications facility. Silviu was just passing through now, but we made a date to meet with him and his boss for dinner in Karachi in a few days.

There seemed a certain irony in the "boys from Braila" both being in Pakistan at the same time. Who could have imagined it, back when we were swimming in the Danube or fighting youthful anti-semites with our wooden swords, that we would be such world travelers? That those young boys would be important experts in the hire of a foreign government?

In fact, when we finally met for dinner, Silviu made an offhand remark about our success in the West. If he had only left Romania years ago, there was no telling what he would have accomplished, he mused.

"Then why did you join the Party," Joyce asked, "instead of getting out like Mark did?"

A frozen silence gripped us for a moment in response to her remark. There had been no challenge in her tone, just an innocent question. Still, I gave her a kick under the table. It was an embarrassing question, at the least, especially with his boss sitting right there, but it also carried a hint of moral judgment that I did not feel. As if by refusing to join the Party and by leaving the country long before him, I had been wiser or morally superior. That was not true.

A complex and thorny knot of emotions surround my experience with Communist Romania. At the bottom of my feelings is a pride that I did not join a political movement that I considered repugnant. Even in the face of countless hardships—not to mention imprisonment—I did not join. When I look back over the past, that decision stands out like a beacon of strength in my character. My resolve was strong. I did not join.

As to whether this was a moral decision or just a consequence of my stubborn personality fixing on an attitude, what does it matter? Was I more or less moral than my parents, who took flight earlier? Should I have taken greater risk to have left the country years before I did? Was

I more or less moral than Georgi, who took up arms against the Communists, and likely sacrificed his life? More or less moral than my friends lured into Party membership by the universal brotherhood slogans of Communism? Was I more or less wise than my friends who joined up because a Party card assured them a job? How do you make such judgments?

Were I to draw any moral line, it would only be to condemn the behavior of those who turned into monsters. Those who used the excuse of ideology to perpetrate crimes. For instance, Nicolae Ceausescu, who slaughtered tens of thousands to further an ideology and his own career, and those like my boyhood friend, Emil, who surrendered his humanity to the Party. That conduct was unforgivable.

* * *

The rest of my nine-month stay in Pakistan was spent setting up the institute. It was quite a chore, less for the actual amount of work involved, than for the attitudes of the Pakistanis with whom I worked. Everything took longer than it should have, especially when I came up against the Pakistani attitude of "*Sabani*," (tomorrow). "We can do that *sabani*." "That will get done *sabani*." "*Sabani* is soon enough." The problem was that *sabani* was more likely to be next week or next year rather than the next day.

Shortly after Joyce and I arrived on campus, we received a beautifully engraved invitation to attend ceremonies at 6 p.m. the next day commemorating the official opening of the university. We arrived at 6 but found no one there, other than a few workers beginning to erect a tent. "Yes, yes," they said. "This tent is for the ceremony. Maybe 10 or 11 o'clock it will be."

We returned at 10:30 to find things slowly getting underway. In the course of the speeches, we learned that these opening ceremonies were supposed to have taken place the previous year, but they had been put off.

In its casual attitude towards time, Pakistan was similar to many less industrialized societies. In countries like the United States, "time is money." We "spend" time, every minute has value. Once spent, it cannot be regained. Pakistanis, on the other hand, had a more elastic notion of time. Time was perceived in large units, a lifetime, a century, eternity. Therefore, a few hours or a year had little value. Some low-level bureaucrats even try to elevate the prestige of their work by taking a long time to make a decision or initiate action.

Joyce and I were so struck by this attitude towards time, that we later wrote an article titled "Time Perception: A Case Study of a Developing Nation" for the journal *Social Focus*. One of the insights we gained was that the time required for a decision is directly proportional to its importance. In taking so long to arrange the opening ceremonies for the university, they were actually demonstrating the importance attached to them. Great things did not happen quickly.

Unfortunately, my Western brain did not work that way, and this time discrepancy caused a few problems in getting done the work of the new research institute. *Sabani* was not soon enough for me. I'm sure my insistence on getting things done expeditiously annoyed my Pakistani workers as much as they sometimes disturbed me. But this cultural friction was a small price to pay to accomplish our goals.

One day I became annoyed at some workers who seemed incapable of getting the floor clean. Given time, they may have gotten the job done properly. But, in frustration I got down on my knees and scrubbed away at the dirt until a piece of the floor was as clean as I wanted it. "That is how you do it," I said. They looked somewhat shocked when I had finished. What I didn't immediately understand was that I had managed to violate another Pakistani cultural norm. This was extraordinary behavior in their class/caste-conscious world, to see their boss doing menial work.

But they weren't nearly as shocked as the University Chancellor and the Grants Director from Islamabad, who chose that very moment to inspect our progress. The director of their research institute scrubbing the floor! It simply wasn't done. It was unthinkable! I growled something about the poor quality of the help who had to be instructed at so simple a task as cleaning the floor.

The bottom line, as far as I was concerned, was that the work got done. Rooms got cleaned, furniture got purchased, a staff hired. And the government was interested in sponsoring some research. By the time my nine-month stay in Pakistan drew to a close, the Sind University Research Institute was a reality.

* * *

Joyce and I had gotten in much travel inside Pakistan. With our servant, we had visited the cities and small villages and gotten a good introduction to the country. But I wanted to introduce Joyce to Europe before we returned to the States. I arranged for the purchase of a Volkswagen and went to Germany to take delivery. While there I met with an old friend from Braila, Karl, who would send us on a dangerous mission that brought me closer than I ever wanted to be to returning to the gulag.

Karl had gotten out of Romania in the 1960s and now lived in Frankfurt. When I told him that Joyce and I would be visiting Romania, he said, "Mark, I have a favor to ask of you." He was retirement age and had worked all his life, he explained. But much of that work had been in Romania. Germany had a retirement program that honored work done in other countries. If he could only get his work record our of Romania, he would be able to retire.

"My mother-in-law has the papers in Bucharest. If you could pick them up and get them back to me . . . " He hesitated, knowing there was a danger. " . . . I would be very grateful." I said that I would.

I was a U.S. citizen now, but tension gripped me when we crossed the border into my old homeland. We had planned a ten day visit. "Planned" is the right word, because visits were only allowed if every stop on your itinerary was meticulously scheduled and paid for in advance. Despite that, we made some impromptu stops.

"Romanian Wedding," was a theater production especially for tourists. It showed actors in traditional folk dress, singing folk songs. We dropped in unannounced, throwing the guides and security people into confusion. But after a check of our papers, they seated us at the table with the Romanian tour guides.

Joyce and I spoke only English in their presence. I did not want to have to explain why I spoke Romanian like a native. It was an amusing ruse, because I could listen in on what the guides were saying about us.

"I'm suspicious of these two," one said. "U.S. passports and a German license plate. I think they're spies."

"Aw, leave them be," the other chided.

After dinner, when people started to dance, one of the guides came up to Joyce and said something in Romanian. Joyce looked confused. "He asked if you wanted to dance," I explained. It was no sooner out of my mouth, then I realized my blunder. I had neatly demonstrated my command of the language. We left in a hurry, before anyone could question me. Obviously, I would not make a very good spy.

Although we made a brief visit to a Black Sea resort, and I played tour guide around Bucharest, we were bored with Romania. "We are being watched," Joyce said again and again, nodding her head in the direction of some suspicious character in our hotel or on the street.

This was not the Romania I remembered. Not the Romania I wanted to remember. What could I show to Joyce that would represent *my* Romania? It was all gone. All that remained was the Romania I hated, the Romania the Communists had created—empty shops, dreary streets, and the cold suspicious faces of its citizens.

After four days, we were ready to leave, eager to be on to our next destination—Italy. We picked up Karl's papers from his mother-in-law, packed the VW, and headed for the Yugoslav border.

I had been tense during the whole of our visit to Romania, but I didn't experience fear until we arrived at the border check point. As they began to dismantle the car—literally—it suddenly occurred to me that the innocent favor we were doing for Karl had put us in danger.

They removed the car seat, then the door panels. If we had been smuggling top-secret documents or contraband, they would have found it. What would they think when they came upon the work documents? It was illegal to remove any official documents without proper authority. Plus, it would arouse their suspicion of greater offenses, namely spying. And when they learned that Karl had left the country illegally, and that I had been a Romanian citizen who also left the country illegally, warning lights would go off in their paranoid imagination, and they would definitely think SPY.

Whether it would embroil us in several days of tedious explanations or involve us in a more serious legal matter, I didn't want to deal with it. I knew only too well how the Romanian legal system worked, and had too many painful memories of my last brush with it. A few of those memories flashed in my mind as the border guards opened our luggage and gave it a thorough once over.

Joyce had placed Karl's papers at the bottom of her large tote bag, just beneath our map. When the guards finished with our suitcases, they started unloading her tote. The pale, strained expression on Joyce's face revealed her own fears. I had told her enough horror stories about Romania, and four days here given her a hint of the repressive atmosphere of the place.

I tried to calm myself and began to compose the "innocent explanation" that I would offer. Joyce's bag was now empty, except for the map at the bottom. The guard reached in his hand, touched the map, and then stopped. As did my heart. Apparently satisfied at that point, he did not remove the map and told us to go ahead.

I must have driven across the bridge to Yugoslavia at 100 kilometers an hour. Safely on the other side, I pulled over to settle myself. "We were lucky," I said to Joyce. "Very lucky." More than a dozen years after I had left, even as a citizen of another country, Romania still had the power to terrorize me.

I know that Joyce appreciated the gravity of our near miss, but I imagine that she experienced it differently than

I did. She had grown up in America in the 1950s and 1960s, nurtured by the freedom and security of that time and place. I came with different baggage. I had seen the freedom and security of my youthful world dissolve under the assault of war and political upheaval. It has left me with a certain political mistrust and insecurity. Unlike many of my American friends, who seem to have been born with a gene for optimism, I believe that the worst of things can happen. Unlike those friends, who possess the conviction that goodness and right always win out, I know that not to be the case.

*   *   *

We spent three months touring Europe. It was a wonderful vacation, but at the back of my mind was always the notion that *I want Joyce to see this.* We must have covered three fourths of Europe, visited the major cities, toured the great buildings, driven through the picturesque landscapes. I felt that I was exposing Joyce to a culture that she had never before experienced, and in the process also showing her something about myself, a product of that European culture.

Joyce's parents joined us for several weeks of our touring, and I felt the same need to show them Europe. Even though I was seeing parts of the continent that I had never seen before, I still felt closer to the heritage of Europe than I did to the heritage of the United States. In the U.S. I was still a newcomer and outsider. I filtered so many of its customs and attitudes through my European experience.

I felt more at home in Europe, and I wanted to reverse the experience for my wife and her family. I wanted them to see a foreign culture and have it alter their exclusively American perception of the world. Joyce had already gotten a small taste of Communist Romania, but I wanted to bring home to them the horrors of World War II, as well. I urged on them a stop at the concentration camp at Dachau. You can't visit there without it leaving a profound impact on you, without it forever altering your perception of humanity.

Inside the camp, Joyce and her parents went their way and I went mine. It is a disturbing place to visit; it should be a required field trip for every school child in the world. When we left Dachau, I had been deeply moved and could see that it had similarly affected the others by the solemn expressions on their faces.

* * *

If Pakistan was a country still struggling mightily to get development under way, Iran was the Middle East success story. Fueled by oil revenues and a progressive Shah, it was attracting a lot of attention in the West. I had been reading articles in the press about Iran's booming economy and how Americans were investing there, when I hit on the idea of visiting Iran to search for research projects.

To say that the board of directors of Northwest Institute of Research was skeptical would be an understatement. They thought I was crazy. What sort of projects was I going to propose to the Iranians? What contacts did I have in Tehran? Of course, the Institute coffers had no funds to subsidize such a long-shot venture.

I understood their skepticism, but I had my father's gambling blood in me. His entrepreneurial philosophy, his voice, seems to echo in me in times of decision. "Attempt it," he would advise. "Money is the cheapest commodity. Take the risk. Better to fail attempting a large venture than succeed at an insignificant one." So, I financed the trip myself from my meager savings, and the directors swore off involvement in any contracts I got from Iran.

Because Joyce was pregnant with our first child, she did not accompany me on this trip. I had decided on a brief stopover in Pakistan to check on the progress of my first foreign venture, since I planned to tout that in Iran as part of my credentials. How had the Research Institute fared without me? What new projects were they involved with?

Arriving at Sind University, I went directly to the Institute offices only to find them empty. A few broken pieces of furniture and some papers scattered about—this was all that remained of Sind University Research Institute. I had the fleeting hope that they had simply changed location, but a visit to the new Chancellor gave me the truth. The people put in charge of the Institute had not followed through on any of the initial projects nor cultivated additional contacts with Islamabad. Employees had been lax about appearing at work, furniture and equipment, had been stolen. The Institute no longer existed.

"We would be happy to have you stay on and rebuild it for us," the Chancellor said. I was not tempted, even for a moment. I thanked him graciously and resumed my trip to Tehran.

14
Taking a Chance in Iran

I arrived in Tehran during Christmas vacation in 1976. Iran was a rapidly developing country thanks to its vast oil reserves and a Shah intent on modernization. Yet, the changes were more than just "modernization." They were far more profound, since they threatened change to the Moslem traditions that were the very foundation of the society.

Outsiders did not yet fully understand the implications of all the changes that were being made in Iran or the complicated forces then stirring in that country. We saw the superficial things. We saw that women were being brought out of the Middle Ages and given rights, and we applauded. We saw that the Shah's secret police, the Savak, repressed political opposition, and we condemned it.

The overall impression for a foreigner visiting Iran in 1976 was that here was a country on the move, taking a bold step into the 20th century. In 1976, most of Iran's enemies lay outside its borders, in Iraq and Afghanistan. And perhaps in the person of one annoying, fundamentalist cleric then living in France, the Ayatollah Khomeini.

I had read about a relatively new university that was rapidly developing and thought that would be a good place to make my first overtures. I had in mind to capitalize on my experience establishing research institutes in the U.S. and in Pakistan, to propose the same thing here. Although I was open to any opportunity that might come my way.

Jundi Shapur University was in the city of Ahwaz. There I met with the chancellor, Dr. Bandiar. We hit it off remarkably well. He had a doctorate in economics from the

Sorbonne and had considerable political clout in Tehran. On this first visit, and on subsequent ones, I was also to find out that he was remarkably well connected.

The university had plans to establish three research institutes in the areas of archeology, hydrology, and computer science. My meetings with Bandiar's staff did not go nearly as well as my meetings with him. His Dean of Science, especially, resisted my involvement. They could do these things on their own, he said, why did they need me? I think he viewed me as someone who might steal some of the glory.

"Don't worry about them," Bandiar told me afterwards. "I make the decisions around here."

I remained in Ahwaz for several weeks, discussing the details of the institutes. Experts would have to be recruited from the West, equipment purchased, contracts negotiated, timetables and logistics worked out. It was an enormous undertaking with an initial budget of $40 million.

I returned home without a contract but highly encouraged. After my return, I purchased a building in Erie to house Northwest Institute of Research. If I was to look respectable enough to have dealings with foreign countries, I should have a real office, not a spare room in my house. Joyce and I went shopping for desks, files cabinets, and typewriters from an army surplus store, and hired a part-time secretary. Though it had a very humble home, NIR now seemed like more of a real institute.

It was about this time that my first daughter, Mara, was born.

* * *

I picked up the three cards I had just been dealt and added them to the pair of jacks I held in my hand, then slowly fanned my cards. A pair of threes had come to join my jacks. Not a bad poker hand, but it only made me nervous. I was in a high-stakes poker game in Ahwaz, Iran, playing with several oil company executives and Chancellor Bandiar, in his lavish home. A sum of money roughly equal to twice my annual salary as a professor stood in stacks before the various players.

I threw a hundred Rial note into the pot. Fortunately the betting was relatively light on that hand or I would have been driven out. I pulled in the pot and took a deep breath. I was playing very conservatively and holding my own. I managed to survive the evening without financial embarrassment. When our poker game drew to a close, the executives were all chauffeured off in their Mercedes, and I was left to marvel about the potential for doing business in Iran.

I was back in the country, this time at the invitation of Dr. Bandiar, staying in his home and being treated like a VIP. Actually, I was being treated as though I already had this multi-million dollar contract, as though we were all partners in Iranian development.

Social functions, such as the poker game, were part of doing business in Iran. Things did not move at an American pace. A social process occurred at the beginning of every deal. It reminded me of my father's dealings in the cattle trade in Romania. Of course, the larger the deal, the more important to get to know the individual with whom you were dealing. Were they trustworthy? Could you work with them?

Bandiar and I continued to develop plans for the research institutes. Facilities, personnel, budgets, equipment, timetables, we sketched these out with increasing detail. Meanwhile, there were people he wanted me to meet and so much that he wanted me to see.

I spent two days on an experimental farm near Ahwaz. Run by a German-trained Iranian, it was a huge project being developed with the cooperation of Israel, Turkey, and Germany. It was curious to see that the interests of development had overridden centuries of animosity between Moslem and Jew. Attitude had begun to change with the Shah's more liberal attitude towards Israel. A relationship that had previously been defined by religion, emphasizing that one seemingly irreconcilable difference, was now being defined by political and economic development. On that issue, Iran and Israel had much in common, not the least of which was how to coax crops from a barren land. On this farm they were experimenting with underground irrigation, with great success. Here was an encouraging example of mutual interest overriding the long-standing religious animosity.

When we sat down to dinner that first night, the Director told me how rewarding it was to work with this type of project. You have the full support of the government. It is an investment for them in economic development. If you do the work, they can be very generous. Sitting in his opulent mansion, attended to by three servants, it was a point well made. My mind was already spinning to come up with an agricultural project to propose to Bandiar. Back home, I knew that Penn State University was very strong in agricultural research. I made a mental note to contact someone there.

* * *

Twice more in 1977 invitations came from Chancellor Bandiar, and I was off to Iran. On each visit I was received like a visiting dignitary, making me increasingly confident of winning the contract. It was apparent that this getting-acquainted period would be long and involved. They seemed to think that I needed to be as familiar and comfortable with Iran and its commerce as it needed to be with me.

On one occasion, I lost my luggage and had to wait in Tehran until I could locate it or purchase new clothing. Although Bandiar was in Ahwaz, he put me up in the mansion that he also maintained in Tehran. His wife took pains to serve me breakfast herself, rather than having the servants do it, an honor accorded important guests.

To entertain me, Bandiar arranged for me to be flown to Isfahan where I was met by a car and driver who took me to see Maidan-i-Shah, the great garden enclosing the royal mosque built by Shah Abbas I in the 16th century.

Meetings were arranged with businessmen in Tehran. Business was good, they told me. Foreign trade was increasing. Their sons were studying engineering and business administration at universities in the United States. They would come home and build a better Iran.

Several of the businessmen asked my assistance in getting sons enrolled at a U.S. college. Perhaps I had connections, they said, perhaps I could arrange such a thing. In fact, on my return home, I did arrange for several of their sons to get admission to Edinboro.

A banquet in my honor was arranged at an exclusive Tehran nightclub, with entertainment provided by a famous singer. She sang beautifully and danced in a skimpy costume, into which the men stuffed huge currency notes. The best of food passed across the table; exorbitantly priced, miniature bottle of whiskey stood before each plate. The evening's bill came to more than $10,000. A trifle for that high-spending crowd.

In Ahwaz, I would stay at Bandiar's house, meet with him during the day to discuss our projects and sip Scotch whiskey with him in the evening. We were becoming good friends.

During the course of all of my visits to Iran, I was greatly impressed by the sheer, raw energy of development. So much needed to be done to modernize the country, and oil was providing the revenue to do it. So many projects were underway or in the planning stage. So many opportunities existed for those with the ideas and initiative, not to mention the patience, to nurture them through the long birthing process.

Resisting this rush to modernization were the various fundamentalist religious factions in the country. Development, they felt, was undermining traditional moslem values. The Communists were also gaining followers in some cities. The Shah had begun to fight these groups with a growing use of his secret police, the Savak.

The spiritual leader of the fundamentalist movement, Ayatollah Khomeini resided in a quiet village in France, but influenced the increasing tensions in Iran. Bandiar and

I never discussed political matters, though that was increasingly on the minds of everyone in 1977.

Of all the trips and meetings that Bandiar arranged for me, none remains more vivid in my mind as that with an Army general, the Iranian military Chief of Staff. We flew from Tehran in a helicopter to a spot near the Afghanistan border, becoming more comfortable and candid with each other as the day progressed.

I had seen the logic of all the other meetings Bandiar had arranged for me. They established social and business contacts or gave me a better understanding of other research projects. But why the General, I wondered. Was Bandiar just looking for excursions to entertain me? Was he trying to demonstrate the depth of his political connections? Or was he attempting to give me the fullest possible picture of the current state of affairs in Iran?

Iran had running border feuds with two of its neighbors in those years, Iraq and Afghanistan. The general took me to a spot on the Afghani border where an enormous number of tanks, artillery, and troops had been massed. We drove past row after row of tanks, their cannons pointed to the east. The general was obviously proud of commanding such an impressive army.

Afghanistan had a pro-Soviet government, Iran a pro-western government. It did not take a genius to grasp that the brewing conflict here was but another stage for playing out the continuing drama of the Cold War.

But on our return trip to Tehran, the general confessed that he was losing more sleep recently over internal matters rather than the chance of foreign conflicts. Social unrest had been spreading to some of the large cities.

"You have enough men and tanks here," I pointed out. "Why don't you shoot the bastards?"

The general chuckled. "The Americans wouldn't like that."

"Do the same for Khomeini. For ten thousand dollars, people would line up for the chance to shoot him."

"You don't understand our relationship with the Americans. We are not free to do what we want, what would be in our own best interest. They are always interfering. They think we should allow our enemies to flourish."

I said, "If you listen to Americans in international politics, you're doomed. The American government doesn't even understand American interests or how to achieve them. The State Department is filled with idiots. They tell others to live by democratic rules, but they never let those rules interfere with what they themselves want to do. I assure you that most Americans also want to see Khomeini dead; they would just not say it openly."

The general gave me a curious look, perhaps surprised that he had set me off like that and that I so openly criticized my adopted country. Perhaps he was also surprised that I so nearly echoed his own feelings on the matter. We didn't explore the issue any further. In minutes we were back in Tehran.

It seemed but the final irony that I would at then be standing in Tehran, in the very place that so well marked America's abandonment of democratic values. In November of 1943, with World War II still raging, Allied leaders Roosevelt, Churchill, and Stalin, met in Tehran to discuss the progress of the war. But the war was quickly overshadowed by questions about the post-war. Stalin made it clear that he intended to incorporate the Baltic States into the Soviet Union. He wanted a Russian sphere of influence.

Although Churchill and Roosevelt were uneasy about such an idea, they did not resist it. They coveted their own parts of Europe. At Tehran, and later at the Yalta conference in February 1945, the post-war division of Europe was arranged. The concessions made to Stalin assured that Eastern Europe would become Communist, that my own country, Romania, would become a puppet state of the Soviet Union.

World War II had left me with a huge reserve of bitterness. It always threatened to well up when given such an opening as my conversation with the General. Whenever I hear talk about governments talking about their motivations or lecturing other governments about how to behave.

Pure and simple, governments act in their own self interest. There is nothing too shocking in that. But they tend to disguise self interest with the propaganda of higher purpose. They do it for the great good of Democracy or for Universal Brotherhood. They have no problem lying for that good cause. Or killing for that good cause. The Romanian Iron Guard terrorized and murdered in the name of God and country, and the Communists killed in the name of ideology. It was the height of hypocrisy for America to tell the Iranians they must show restraint in the face of their enemies.

I should have said to the general back then, "Beware of those who always speak of values, who always criticize others for lacking values; they are the ones who have no values of their own, the ones you can not trust." The IRA, the Ku Klux Klan, the Mujahadein will bomb you, burn you, or slit your throat with the name of God on their lips.

Over the few tumultuous years that followed that helicopter trip, I often recalled my conversation with the general. He would have more than enough enemies to battle in the coming years.

*   *   *

The ringing of the telephone woke me. I was in my bed, in Erie, PA. The alarm clock read 11:30. Who would be calling?

"Mark, I am in Philadelphia. They have left me alone in a hotel room for the weekend with nothing to do." It was Chancellor Bandiar. He was visiting the University of Pennsylvania. "Can you come and get me? I don't want to give these people my projects."

I hastily recruited a colleague from Edinboro as a travelling companion and covered the 450 miles from Erie to Philadelphia in record time, arriving before dawn at Bandiar's hotel. We loaded his luggage and were back on the road before sunrise. I don't know if he had been seeking a proposal from the University of Pennsylvania on the same projects I hoped to win, but I felt as though I had snatched victory from my competitors.

They had simply deposited Bandiar in his hotel room, without a host or any diversions, as though he were a traveling salesman in town for a few days. He was offended by the treatment. He was alone in a foreign country on an important mission and he expected the sort of lavish hospitality that he had accorded me when I visited Iran. Instead, he got a lonely hotel room.

It was curious that when we stopped on the road for breakfast, Bandiar ordered my friend about, assuming that he was my servant. How much of a shock would it be for him to see my way of life?

Bandiar settled into a room in my house. By his standards, these were modest accommodations indeed, no mansion, no servants. But we extended to him simple curtesies, such as having his favorite cigarettes set out for him, having Joyce personally serve his breakfast, in the Iranian fashion of accommodating an honored guest. I thought it best not to show him NIR's one-room office, but I did gather together NIR's board of directors, so that he might see the people behind my organization.

Although my humble research institute could hardly muster the resources and facilities of organizations affiliated with major universities, I had a better feel for how to do business with officials from foreign countries because I better understood their culture. Maybe these are lessons learned from my father, maybe it comes from growing up as part of a European culture, which had a different attitude towards business than that found at your modern business schools.

For the most part, I simply entertained him, as he had done so wonderfully for me when I was in his country. For several days, we played the tourist. I took him to visit Niagara Falls and showed him everything there was to see in the Erie area. One evening, as we sat on my back porch sipping scotch, Bandiar said, "Let's talk business, Mark."

Yes, it was time. We had gotten to know each other, learned about the other's needs and capabilities, their style and way of doing business. We had visited each other's country, met family and friends, and shared opinions on many subjects. Now, we felt comfortable enough with each other to work together on our projects.

The details were few. The terms of the agreement were already understood by both of us. We outlined what our next steps would be, we shook hands, and he assured me he would send out a formal contract after his return to Iran. True to his word, it arrived in the mail a few weeks later. Forty million dollars looked like a very great deal of money when written in a contract. That was the figure for this first phase of the project, to cover all the preliminary work of establishing the institutes.

The day the contract arrived, I called Joyce first, then each of the NIR directors, to crow about the victory. This contract would give NIR major credibility plus provide the income to establish it as a viable institution. But just as satisfying for me was the sense of vindication and power I felt. I had taken a risk, just like my "gambling" father would have done. Although this was the biggest roll of the dice I had ever taken, it was certainly not an isolated case. Before and since winning that contract, I have gone out on a limb many times. When it works out, I appear clever, when it doesn't, I appear stupid. If I didn't fail so much, I'd worry that I wasn't trying hard enough, taking sufficient risk. But this Iranian contract shone as a clear and satisfying victory.

I have come to believe that this entrepreneurial spirit is a particular quality of immigrants, that it blossoms in their personality as soon as they arrive on the fertile soil of opportunity in the West. They work hard and save money to improve life for themselves and their families. And they start businesses. Almost every day, you read in the press about some immigrant who worked two jobs for many years, saving his money until he had enough to start a business or to buy the foundering shop where he had worked many years as a clerk.

It seems curious that immigrants are often the object of criticism in America. They are a drain on the economy. They are stealing Americans' jobs. What nonsense. Immigrants have always been the life blood of the American economy. They do menial jobs Americans do not want to do. And they often edge out Americans in competing for good jobs.

There are certainly many hard-working Americans, but so many Americans seem obsessed with security or self indulgence. I am shocked to see even young people so concerned with feathering their retirement accounts. The security of a civil service position is the dream of many college graduates. They want to retire at age 55. For Americans the accumulation of money has become an *end* in itself, and the risk-taking, entrepreneurial spirit is becoming a thing of the past. Their lives have been too good and too safe, and so their worst fear has been that they might lose the good life.

*   *   *

My advertisements for experts in computer technology, hydrology, and archeology began appearing in professional publications. The salaries were handsome, and they would be given the chance to work with large budgets and the latest technology. Resumes began piling up on my desk. People within these professions began to wonder. What is this Northwest Institute of Research in Erie, Pennsylvania? Who is this Dr. Iutcovich that he has so much money to spend?

We were moving first with the computer institute. I sought bids on huge computer systems, all the latest technology, and interviewed some of the best talent in the country. Quickly, a level of excitement was building around the project. In essence, I would be working with a clean slate and a blank check to establish a world-class computer institute.

Meanwhile, in Iran, protests against the Shah were becoming more frequent, and in France, the Ayatollah Khomeini becoming more outspoken in his criticism. But the projects remained on course. Chancellor Bandiar and I exchanged letters and phone calls to monitor progress.

Finally, in mid-1978 I dispatched a computer expert to Iran to meet with Bandiar. They would iron out further details on purchases and schedules. Surprisingly, he was not well received. After waiting for weeks without success to meet with the Chancellor, he was asked to leave the country. I sent letters asking for an explanation, and tried to get through phone calls, all without success.

I got my explanation instead on the evening news. In the fall, violent protests against the Shah erupted in Iran. In September, 12 cities came under marshall law. I wondered what my friend the general was doing now. Moving his tanks and troops from the eastern border to the cities, no doubt. Losing much sleep.

Unrest turned into a revolution that would not be contained. On January 16, 1979, the Shah fled the country, and later that same month Khomeini made his triumphant return. Iran was reborn as a fundamentalist, religious state. All western connections were severed. Overnight, my 40 million dollar contract became just so much worthless paper. Hostages were taken in the American embassy. For more than a year, they would galvanize American attention and keep tension between the U.S. and Iran on full boil. They would also occupy the time and attention of President Jimmy Carter and eventually consume his presidency.

So many times during that long ordeal, I recalled the words of that Iranian general complaining that the Americans were intent on letting Iran's enemies flourish. The State Department and the American government had succeeded. They had done their part to put Khomeini in power. Now Iran's enemies were our enemies. My enemies. I was left to reflect that once more in my tangled history, the swift and violent overthrow of a government had redirected the course of my life.

A few months after the fall of Iran, I received a letter from Chancellor Bandiar. He had gotten out of the country and was now living with his family in France. He just wanted to inform me that he was safe and thank me for my efforts.

I wondered how much advance planning Bandiar had put into his move. I knew that his wife and family had been in France before the Revolution. Perhaps he had seen the inevitable well in advance and made preparations. I thought of my parents, stopping in Paris for a time after fleeing Romania, how lost they had felt and how uncertain of what the future held for them. I thought of the sea of immigrants cast about the world because of war, politics, economics, and religion.

I mailed a check to Bandiar, a respectable sum that I hoped would help to make his transition easier. I sent it to the address on his letter, but it came back undelivered.

*   *   *

Sometimes it seems ironic to juxtapose personal events next to national tragedies. What meaning do you give to the happenings in one life, when a country is in the throes of revolution? Still, as a landmark in my life, an event occurred just about the time that Iran was coming apart.

Puica called me at home. The tone of her voice—strained, over-wrought—struck a chord, instantly recalling the arguments we used to have back when we lived together in Bucharest, back when we used to break up our relationship and rekindle it as often as the seasons changed.

But some other quality lurked in her voice as well, something darker. She may have been drunk. "I hear that you have a baby now," she said, in a voice choked with emotion.

"Yes," I said. "A girl. We named her Mara."

"Mark, Mark . . . All those years ago . . . things could have gone a different way for us . . . ." She was sobbing.

"Puica. Are you all right?"

"I should congratulate you. Is she a pretty child?"

"Yes."

"Well, that's why I called. I'm happy for you."

I had no words for the moment, and I was frightened for her. I must have been babbling towards the end. "Things work out . . . time changes things . . . I hope you will be happy, too." I forget which platitudes came to my lips.

"I hope you appreciate how lucky you are, Mark. I hope you know that. Not everyone is blessed."

The instant she hung up, I telephoned my cousin in Montreal and told him about the call, how distressed Puica sounded. Would he please run over and check on her, I asked.

An hour or so later, he called me back from Puica's apartment. "Mark. I sent for the ambulance, but I think it's too late. She took pills or something. I don't know."

A few days later, I traveled to Montreal for her funeral. Puica had never married, but had some close friends, and had brought her sister to Montreal, as well. Financially, she had done well for herself. She had maintained a second apartment in New York, thanks to the success of her psychiatric practice.

I left Montreal with a small table Puica had kept in her apartment. I had given it to her. Sometimes I am more of a romantic than I would care to accept. The tangle of emotions I felt for Puica and for what we had shared gripped me powerfully as she went into the ground. I ached at losing her, as if an important piece of my past had been taken away.

What is it in this immigrant experience that makes me want to hold onto pieces of that other life, like souvenirs of a place I had once visited? A moment, a story, an attitude from the past sometimes seems so substantial compared to the ephemera of my day-to-day life. Maybe it is just a natural response to aging, but it plants the idea in my head that something valuable has been lost. That time has eroded rich layers of experience.

Maybe it is just that time has eroded the ephemera of the past and left standing the solid skeleton. When I search my memory now it is only these bones that emerge to indicate the underlying structure of my life.

15
Epilogue

The hour was late. The coffee in my cup was cold. I had yet to prepare my classroom lecture for tomorrow. I sat at a desk in the one-room office of the Northwest Institute of Research doing a final check on a research report. Tomorrow was the deadline, so the work had to be done. The secretary had gone home for the night long ago. She was probably in bed by now, which is where I should have been. But I flipped the page and continued reading. My commitment to Northwest Institute of Research had given my life new direction.

To talk only about the Iranian contract in the history of NIR gives a false picture. I certainly missed those glamorous days of huge budgets and high living in Iran, when it seemed that the world would so quickly open its bounty to us. But what became clear following the Iranian Revolution was that if NIR was to ever be a success, it would not come overnight.

Instead, it would survive on a diet of small projects—a few thousand dollars to do a marketing study or process some computer work. I traveled to Washington looking for federal projects, without success. We applied for many projects but got only a few. Much of the work fell to Joyce and me.

By the late 1970s there were probably more reasons to close down NIR than to keep it going. We made no money from the work. It was not some lofty scholarly endeavor that demanded our sacrifice. Nor did it help to advance our academic careers.

Several factors kept me committed to the survival of the organization. I cannot discount the simple, bull-headed stubbornness that is a part of my nature. Once I undertake a project, I must see it through, sometimes even when logic suggests otherwise. I can't help thinking that nothing so well paves the way to success, however you wish to define that elusive term, as simple, dogged persistence.

A stronger motivation was my complete faith in the viability of the NIR. For one, I knew that the research skills I had acquired during my education as a sociologist had commercial value. Many of the projects NIR undertook used the broad academic skills of research, analysis, and interpretation.

I also believed that sociology had a unique perspective to offer in explaining social issues. By broadening the focus of analysis, by examining the larger context of a problem, insights could be gained that wouldn't otherwise reveal themselves.

I shouldn't discount as a third factor for persevering with the organization the fact that Joyce and I enjoyed the work. It was exciting. We studied the workings of the criminal justice system and the effectiveness of an alcohol and drug treatment center. We assessed the environmental and archeological impact of construction projects. What was the viability of automatic bank teller machines or a local TV cable franchise? We were up to our elbows in so many of the social and political issues of the moment, as well as new trends in the economy. We enjoyed being part of the action.

So, we persisted. When our first office burned, we moved to equally humble quarters across the street, and continued. When the Internal Revenue Service informed us that as a non-profit organization, we could not undertake certain types of projects, such as political polling, we established a second, for-profit, institute and called it Keystone University Research Corporation (KURC). And we continued.

In 1985, we bought an abandoned school building and moved our research institutes to their current location on

West 17th Street in Erie. There was much activity, and reason to be optimistic that growth was just around the corner, but financially, this was the low point. We were holding on, surviving, but just barely. Each month we accumulated more bills than income. We were constantly holding our breath, waiting for some last-minute check to arrive to cover our obligations.

Finally, there dawned one of those fateful days, when you knew some momentous decision loomed that could change your life. I visited the bank, and stated the problem with my usual directness, "You have two choices. Either loan me enough money to get through this difficulty, or call your lawyer right now and declare me bankrupt." We got the money, we continued, and we grew.

As our capabilities and reputation grew, so did the list of our clients. It came to include retail stores, corporations, local and state governments, labor unions, colleges, military bases. Of course, we did not have experts in all these areas on staff, we hired them as the need arose for the duration of the project.

As we took on larger and larger projects, the workload grew as well. I continued teaching at Edinboro (which had become a university), and Joyce was now on the faculty of Villa Maria College. Our second child, Nadia, had been born. On top of the busy duties of parenting, both of us maintained an academic career and worked as an executive with the research institutes.

Colleagues at Edinboro University would ask, "Why do you work so hard?" Sometimes it was said with a tone of envy, but more often with complete incomprehension. After all, I was a full professor, with tenure and a comfortable salary. I attended professional conferences and published the occasional scholarly article. So, why did I knock myself out seeking research grants and traveling to foreign countries looking for work?

I think I have always been an enigma for the institution at which I worked. Letters in the campus newspaper have criticized me. Rumors have circulated. What is Iutcovich up to? I recall that after I returned from Pakistan, a persistent rumor made the rounds on campus that I had stolen 14 million dollars from the Pakistani government. How this originated, I have no idea. I would joke about it, claiming that I had really stolen $14,750,000. And $750,000 is not peanuts.

Something of a mystique had grown up around me. I did not neatly fit the mold of Edinboro professors. I was a foreigner. I had been educated in another country. In my colorful past, I'd had scrapes with Nazis and Communists and been imprisoned in a gulag. I stole money from foreign governments and rescued Iranian officials in late-night escapades. My research institutes had contracts with who knew what government agencies and which foreign countries. Those so inclined to see mystery in my personality had ample ammunition. Those wishing to report me as a spy to the FBI might have detailed a list of suspicious behavior.

Because I had a different background and a different outlook on life, my colleagues didn't understand my behavior. That lack of understanding sometimes led them to form negative opinions about me. Here was yet another lesson in my long education as an immigrant. If you didn't fit the standard model of behavior for your position, you risked the suspicion, the poor opinion, even the enmity of your colleagues.

My tense relationship with the college administration also continued. They had not been pleased when I established my own research institute, thus depriving them of the 10 percent administrative fee they had been collecting. However, we had continued a business relationship. Because of a contract I had with the county government to keep tax assessments, I needed the use of the college's large computer, and was paying $12,000 a year to rent time on it. I scheduled time only in the evening and hired my own operator, so the arrangement was certainly advantageous for the college.

At one point in the early 1980s, one of the vice presidents came to me and said that the college wanted to increase the rent for the computer to $20,000, almost the entire sum I was getting from the contract. I was outraged. It struck me as nothing short of robbery. I met with the president but got no satisfaction. Sometimes necessity helps you to make difficult decisions. That was certainly the case here. I was forced to borrow $85,000 to purchase a mainframe computer large enough to handle the work. And so, another rift had opened between me and the administration, and KURC had dramatically increased its capabilities, and its debt.

As I have gotten older, I have not gained any tolerance for the foolishness of bureaucracies. And I was not very tolerant to begin with. But at the core of the tension that has persisted between the administration and my colleagues and me is the fact that I "work." That is, I work at something in addition to teaching.

For me it is the most natural of connections. I teach research methods in the classroom, and practice it on the job. I teach about the *applied* aspect of Sociology and demonstrate its myriad applications through my research institute. Nothing could better prepare me for the classroom than rolling up my sleeves and practicing what I teach. Nothing more fully exposes me to new developments in the field and allows me to test theories and determine their usefulness, than to be wrestling with this work day in and day out.

Too often in academia, professors only teach and theorize about their chosen field without actually practicing it. This increases the likelihood that they will lose touch with new developments and never be forced to deal with the countless practical difficulties faced by "working" professionals.

For me, the institutes have been an outlet for professional growth. Although my education had been more in theoretical sociology, I had, through my work, become thoroughly involved in applied sociology, using the research tools of sociology to gain knowledge that had a practical application that could be immediately applied to evaluate or solve a problem.

Coincidentally, interest in applied sociology was also growing within the academic community at this time. The Society for Applied Sociology (SAS) began to emerge in northeast Ohio during the late 1970s, and was officially incorporated in 1984. Joyce knew one of the founding members, Alex Boros, from Kent State. Through her, I became involved. The Society's goal of demonstrating "the utility of sociological perspectives in solving problems of community life," so closely matched our own work at NIR and KURC.

Joyce and I collaborated on many research and publishing projects during these years. Through her encouragement, I became more deeply involved in SAS. In 1986 we brought SAS's annual conference to Edinboro University, and the following year I was elected as president of the society and helped to further establish the organization in those formative years. In a sense, my "work" had merged more fully with my profession. *Applied* Sociology had taken on a more formal academic standing, and Joyce and I have since written articles and published a book on the role of the sociologist as consultant.

Beyond providing for professional growth, Keystone University Research Corporation has become wonderfully successful. In 1987, the federal government created the President's Commission on Privatization. Its study of government operations concluded that great advantages could be gained by utilizing the creative talents and ingenuity of the private sector to perform some of the functions then done by government.

Following the Commission's advice, many state governments began to seek contracts with private-sector organizations. KURC acquired several large, multi-year contracts from Pennsylvania to administer a variety of state programs. We met the challenge of providing the same level of service formerly offered by the state, but for considerably less money. More than 40 people now work for the organization and for the job skill training school we established.

All the while that Joyce and I were achieving success in our professional collaboration, we had a more important private collaboration, as well—our family. No experience in the past 40 years has made a more profound impact on me than being a "family man."

* * *

I recall an occasion a couple years after the birth of my second daughter, Nadia. I was sitting with her and her older sister Mara, in the audience at Joyce's graduation ceremony when she earned her Ph.D. from Kent State University. I was understandably proud of Joyce. She had so well balanced the demands of family and her studies. Now she would embark on a career in academia.

It was the 1970s, a time of dramatic change in women's social roles. I remember thinking that Mara and Nadia were fortunate to have Joyce as their role model. In fact, they were fortunate to have two parents who would demonstrate to them the important values of hard work and independent thinking. Valuing education as we did, I imagined that we would well prepare these children for the world.

Despite busy schedules, we took time to do things together as a young family. We had great summer adventures driving a motorhome across country, sharing the many experiences of our nomad vacations. In some ways, it reminded me of my family when I was very young—before all the terrors came. I felt the same powerful bonds of love and security. We were our own little group at the center of the universe, and I wanted that precious time to stretch on indefinitely. Secure in my own life, I imagined that I could protect my daughters from any modern-day terrors.

As the years have passed, I have spent much time worrying about my children's future. Most parents worry about their child making it in the world. The world changes, dangers lurk. How do you protect and prepare your child to deal with them? Joyce and I occasionally came into conflict over how to raise our daughters, a conflict between American values and what, for lack of a better term, I'll call "Old World" values.

In my youth, the importance of family was stressed over and over. Nothing was stronger than the bond between parents and children, between siblings. Obligation to and reliance upon a larger, extended family bound us in a supporting web of human contacts. A certain behavior was expected of children, including great curtesy to their elders and respect for their parents. The pattern of expectations and responsibility placed upon children seemed to hold the world firm.

But in America, so many outside distractions pull at the fabric of the family. The media and our culture in general glamorize behavior that undermines family cohesiveness. It is the natural course of things in America to have children grow up fast and to allow them great latitude in their behavior. We seem to accept the fact that outside forces will control their behavior more than the guidance of family or tradition.

This is hard for me to accommodate. I often bemoan American permissiveness, believing that its lack of limits and fixed boundaries does not serve children, or the rest of us, very well. But it is nearly impossible for a parent to stand alone against all the contrary messages conveyed by our culture.

Of course, the home is a reflection of attitudes that exist elsewhere in society. The same climate of permissiveness seen in the family, pervades our entertainment, legal system, and government. It has also taken firm root in our educational system, the other place where we might expect our children to acquire the necessary skills to deal with life.

Education alone is not responsible for all the challenges facing our society; it is constructed by the requirements of the larger society. But, since I am an educator, and also a parent, I have seen first hand the workings of our educational system and the changes that have come about in it in the past few decades. My concern about those changes touches directly on some of the issues I have raised in this book.

I recall when we had sent one of our daughters off to a private school in another state. She roomed with two other girls, one of Chinese immigrant parents. The school was very demanding, and at the end of the first year all three girls had had enough and did not want to return the following year. We withdrew our daughter from the school, as did the parents of the other American girl. The Chinese parents, however, told their daughter she was staying. Period. Yes, the school was hard, they agreed, but that was precisely why they wanted her to be there. So, she stayed.

Unlike many American parents, immigrants do not expect the school system to single-handedly educate their children. There are many good schools, but children have to be motivated to learn, they have to see that learning is valued.

Unfortunately what they typically see being honored is sports. The sports culture is pervasive and powerful. By the time children can walk, there are leagues in which they compete. Parents run them around to tennis class and little league.

Many days I rise before dawn to drive my teenage daughter to her swimming lessons. She is on the school team, a good competitor, and I admire her dedication and discipline in sticking to her training, even when it requires such pre-dawn practice. But, I can't help but wonder what child or parent would make such a sacrifice for an academic pursuit. Would they rise at 5 a.m. to spend time studying for an exam? to spend an extra hour in a library or to train with the debate society?

If this is an unrealistic expectation of any adolescent, shouldn't we expect a better attitude from schools and parents? And yet, the high school that can't afford teacher training workshops, the latest textbooks, or sufficient computers is able to find the money to buy new football uniforms or to transport the entire baseball team hundreds of miles away for an out-of-town competition. Sports equal money, and Values always follow money.

The football coach is usually the most highly paid person on a university campus, sometimes earning more than the university president or any nobel laureate who happens to be on the faculty. Student athletes are given full scholarships and other benefits as well. Their efforts on the playing field elevate them to hero status on campus. The fortunate few who make it into professional sports can look forward to earning salaries in excess of those paid to corporate CEO's or the President of the United States.

We have gotten distracted from our basic educational priorities. We train and entertain young people rather than educating them. Instead of asking whether they will be educated or will be able to think rationally to deal with the vicissitudes of life, students ask, "What job can I get with this degree?" We have lost sight of what education should be.

Acquiring job skills is not "education," and yet at so many of our schools we have brought vocational preparation to the top of the agenda. This may prepare our youth for work but it does not prepare them for life.

To be educated means to possess sufficient knowledge and the basic critical skills to make rational decisions. It means being infused with an enthusiasm for life-long learning and with the curiosity to pursue your interests and the discipline to accept your responsibilities.

Individuals who lack these skills are more vulnerable to manipulation. Unable to analyze and solve difficult problems, they seek the easy solution. They generalize, find scapegoats, and turn a sympathetic ear to the nearest demagogue who promises a quick fix. Unable to think for themselves, they embrace an ideology. I am Conservative or I am Liberal, they proudly assert. I am a Born Again Christian. I am a Skinhead. Nothing more strongly reminds me of the worst impulses of Romania's experience with Nazism and Communism than the capitulation of its citizens to an ideology.

This drift towards ideological affiliation is one of the most dangerous trends prevalent in America today. And once we begin to accept this brand of thinking, we set up the possibility of political and social disaster. Forgive me if that sounds like the ravings of the unwashed. Sometimes

I feel that for the rest of my life I will be looking for Nazis and Communists beneath every rock. Still, the lesson is clear—the freedoms we enjoy can only be guarded by a free-thinking populace.

Mindless and dangerous ideologies can come from any point on the political compass, but it is my growing concern over the rise of the political right in America that has motivated me to get involved in the political system.

This is all sounding so very much like preaching. I thought I would not be doing much of that in my memoirs. But the temptation is great, and I am only human. As an academic, I analyze facts and look for explanations. I try to make sense of the muddle of my own life and fit it into the larger picture of history and society. The temptation is to apply those revelations about self to the larger population. As with my entrepreneurial ventures, sometimes I am right and appear wise, and sometimes off the mark and look the fool.

* * *

In 1985, a friend approached me to do a political poll. He was running for the state legislature and wanted to gauge voter support and their opinion on various issues. I conducted the poll for him, and supported him for office, which he won.

I had conducted political polls before, but this one marked a turning point for me and led to my deeper involvement in politics. Since then, I have actively supported numerous other candidates for office. I have more carefully watched the political scene. I have conducted polls at my own expense, given generously to various campaigns, hosted fund-raising dinners at my house, and been consulted on campaign strategy.

One strong motivation for my deeper interest in politics has been my professional work. After all, a sociologist studies social issues, often the same social issues that preoccupy voters. KURC has conducted studies and been actively involved in such areas as crime, unemployment, education, health services, and the environment.

In some of these areas, I have seen the same problems persist for decades, even when solutions seemed obvious. I have seen the machinations of government often contribute more to the continuation of these problems than to their solutions. One can't view such things so closely without building up a reservoir of frustration and aching for the clear-headed, practical solutions that so often remain just outside our reach.

My passion for politics also springs from the deeper well of the past. In my youth I once dreamed of a political career. There seemed to be no end of social problems in my native Romania awaiting solutions. But my only elected office was as president of Romanian university students in 1947. The advent of communism cut short my political ambitions.

Because my life has been so profoundly influenced by politics. Because I have seen such tidal shifts of government, and suffered their repercussions, it has made me more sensitive to the emergence of ideological thinking and more fearful of the consequences of indifference to that thinking. It has also made me more impatient with loud programs that take us no closer to solving persistent problems.

My increasing involvement in politics over the past decade coincides with my rising concern for conditions in America. To put it bluntly: The same disturbing developments that ushered in Nazism and Communism in Romania are prevalent in American today.

I know full well that messages like this sound like wild-eyed doomsaying in America. The hair-shirt prophet with his placard warning that "The End is near," is a standard character in our cartoons, an alarmist who warns of a danger that never appears. So, let me make no predictions, but only mention facts and observations. Let me tell you what ghosts haunt me most from my past.

In the 1930s a movement emerged in Romania called the Iron Guard whose avowed goal was to restore the former glory of Romania. Like much of the world, Romania suffered under an economic Depression in the 1930s, giving the slogan of restored national greatness much appeal. The Iron Guard, whose official name was the League of the Archangel Michael, gained solid support in the population as a patriotic, Christian movement. They spoke of the old fashioned values of country, family, heritage, and faith that Romania had once possessed.

It was the Communists who had brought about our problems, they said, and so measures were taken against them. They were harassed, beaten, their political party outlawed. Then we were told that the real cause of our problems were the Jews. They were not of our country; they were leeches, siphoning off our wealth, our very life's blood. They were harassed, beaten, and murdered. Any citizen who resisted this program was against Romania and God and risked suffering the same abuse.

Not coincidentally, at this time the Nazi Party was rising to power in Germany, preaching the same message. Restoring national greatness was not for the faint of heart, but this was the Lord's work and thus justified any extreme to purify and elevate the country. For those who saw that our problems were great and the causes complex, it was comforting to think that the solution could be so simple.

At the close of World War II, when the Nazi ideology of restored national greatness looked as bankrupt as the Romanian treasury, Communism came to my country. The Communists were every bit as efficient and ruthless as the Nazis at imposing their will. Murder all who resisted, all who disagreed, or who might potentially disagree. Enemies to the cause were everywhere. It required extraordinary vigilance. Those who thought, rather than believed, were enemies. Watch them, imprison them, break their will, eliminate them. The cause was too great to suffer the distraction of non-believers.

Oh, the slogans we heard. Oh, the high values of brotherhood and social equality that were extolled to justify every atrocity. Big promises that were too good to be true, too fantastic to be believed. But, believing required less risk than thinking. And years later, when every slogan trumpeted even more loudly with fantasy and lies, it was too late; the land overflowed with "true believers."

It is the current crop of "true believers" in America who scare me. Every cause seems to have its fanatics who believe anything is justified. Opponents of abortion burn clinics and shoot doctors. People who have a beef with the government kill federal agents or blow up an office building. Racists burn black churches.

To hide the true nature of their cause, any group need only claim divine legitimacy. Racist and neo-Nazi groups give themselves such names as Christian Patriots Defense League, Arizona Priests, Americas Promise Ministries, Identity Church Movement. Less "notorious" movements, such as the Christian Coalition, use similar tactics to impose their agendas. In the face of scientific evidence, they force school districts to teach creationism and use only those textbooks that have their seal of approval.

It is hard to oppress or kill someone with logic, but easy to do it in the name of religion.

Americans, who pride themselves on finding practical solutions to their problems, have surrendered their minds to faith and ideology. It is far easier to believe than to think, far more satisfying to vent anger than to struggle with difficult problems. It is the "believers" who always talk about Values and who always find someone else to blame, persecute, or kill.

The approach of fanatics is simple. They look at a problem—say, the increase in violent crime in America—and rather than think through possible solutions, they cling mindlessly to an ideology. They join the National Rifle Association, for instance. The solution to violent crime is to put guns in the hands of more people, to allow citizens to own assault weapons or bullets that penetrate bullet-proof vests, or plastic guns that escape detection in security equipment. Logic will not turn them from their faith, nor will the desperate pleas of police officers who have to face the arsenals of criminals, nor the mounting statistics on accidental shootings.

Earlier in this book I promised to resist the temptation to lecture. Instead, I said that I wished to find the connection between the individual who lived in Romania during those early years and the individual writing this book. I have found some of those connections. Individuals have left their mark on my personality, and experiences of the past still resonate in my thinking.

In my youth, I saw America from afar; in my adulthood I have often held a magnifying glass to different parts of American society. Two very different perspectives yet they possess a disturbing connection. The present reminds me of the past.

Because my family was prosperous, and my father had important connections, I felt somewhat immune from the political turmoil of my youth. Even when evil began to touch friends and family, it was still possible to think of those occurrences as isolated incidents. We had a well-ordered society, with sturdy traditions of justice.

But, to see the rise of Romania's Nazi Iron Guard, to see a fascist government in power, and then the Communist takeover that would so completely destroy the Romania that once existed, makes me believe that the worst can happen if it is allowed to happen.

So, today when I see America's drift towards the political far right, when I see people like Jerry Falwell, Pat Robertson, Louis Farrakhan, and Pat Buchanan, and a host of others, trying to dictate our political agenda, I take notice.

When immigrants are blamed for stealing jobs, rather than for creating them and vitalizing the economy, it smacks of a scapegoat mentality. When religious groups call for a Constitutional amendment to put prayer in the school and in general seek to make social policy a matter of faith, I experience the most unsettling sort of *deja vu*.

Those social reformers that so dearly want to save our souls and our national greatness, have just the opposite effect. Their message of intolerance creates a subculture of True Believers. Though they may represent themselves as the champions of democracy, they are really the enemies of democracy. They seek to limit discourse rather than encourage it. That leads to a shrinking of our freedoms, a closing of our society and our minds.

When a segment of the population thinks that it knows all the answers—especially when they have received the truth from the lips of God—and can justify radical means to achieve its goals, we are on the doorstep of repression and decline. America deserves better than that. Because America has given me so much, I feel that my responsibility now is to support a climate of tolerance. If there is further greatness to be achieved, that is the only way to achieve it.